Education and Ontario Family History

GENEALOGIST'S REFERENCE SHELF

Education and Ontario Family History

A Guide to Resources for Genealogists and Historians

MARIAN PRESS

DUNDURN PRESS
TORONTO

Editor: Ruth Chernia
Copy Editor: Allison Hirst
Designer: Jennifer Scott
Printer: Marquis

Library and Archives Canada Cataloguing in Publication

Press, Marian
       Education and Ontario family history : a guide to the resources for genealogists and historians / by Marian Press.

(Genealogist's reference shelf)
Co-published by Ontario Genealogical Society.
Includes bibliographical references and index.
Issued also in electronic format.
ISBN 978-1-55488-747-7

1. Education--Ontario--History--Sources. 2. Ontario-- Genealogy--Handbooks, manuals, etc. I. Ontario Genealogical Society II. Title. III. Series: Genealogist's reference shelf

LA418.O6P75 2011   370.9713   C2010-902695-0

1   2   3   4   5   15   14   13   12   11

 Conseil des Arts
du Canada
Canada Council
for the Arts
 Canadä
 ONTARIO ARTS COUNCIL
CONSEIL DES ARTS DE L'ONTARIO

We acknowledge the support of the Canada Council for the Arts and the Ontario Arts Council for our publishing program. We also acknowledge the financial support of the Government of Canada through the Canada Book Fund and Livres Canada Books, and the Government of Ontario through the Ontario Book Publishers Tax Credit program, and the Ontario Media Development Corporation.

Care has been taken to trace the ownership of copyright material used in this book. The author and the publisher welcome any information enabling them to rectify any references or credits in subsequent editions.

J. Kirk Howard, President

Printed and bound in Canada.
www.dundurn.com

Ontario Genealogical Society
Suite 102, 40 Orchard View Boulevard
Toronto, Ontario, Canada M4R 1B9
tel. (416) 489-0734   fax. (416) 489-9803
provoffice@ogs.on.ca   www.ogs.on.ca

Dundurn Press	Gazelle Book Services Limited	Dundurn Press
3 Church Street, Suite 500	White Cross Mills	2250 Military Road
Toronto, Ontario, Canada	High Town, Lancaster, England	Tonawanda, NY
M5E 1M2	LA1 4XS	U.S.A. 14150

For Stuart
(1945–2002)

CONTENTS

Introduction   9

Chapter 1   Where the Resources Reside   13
Chapter 2   Students in Ontario Schools   36
Chapter 3   Schools   68
Chapter 4   Teachers and Teaching   94
Chapter 5   Curriculum and Textbooks   141
Chapter 6   Post-Secondary Education   154

Appendix: Schoolhouse Museums in Ontario   163
Additional Works Consulted   167

INTRODUCTION

It would be the rare family historian with Ontario ancestors who could claim no need to research educational records; most residents of the province experienced at least some schooling and many, both male and female, worked as teachers, even if just for a brief period. Historical educational resources, such as school registers and annual lists of practising teachers, may therefore be useful to the genealogist in charting an ancestor's whereabouts over time and adding to the knowledge gained from more standard sources, such as vital records and census records. The record that actually names an ancestor in the educational system may be missing, but the history of a local school — many of which have been written over the years — can provide a clear picture of what life was like for a pupil or a teacher for those interested in their own wider family history.

An even broader perspective on what nineteenth and early twentieth-century schooling was like can be found in the many records available describing school curricula and the textbooks approved for use in the schools. The information provided in this book, therefore, goes beyond the sources that just provide lists of names (although these are the sources that are emphasized), and, as a result, it is hoped that the information gathered here will also be useful for those undertaking a more general study of the history of education in Ontario.

Education has been defined here as that which begins with what we would now understand as elementary education and continues to education at the university level. The records of professional institutions, such as business, medicine, law, and theology schools, have not been included, although the discussion on who holds the records for the universities would also apply to many of these schools. I also have not included French-language schooling in Ontario and Aboriginal residential schools.

Although "Ontario" is a relatively recent term for the province, for simplicity's sake, Ontario is the name that I have principally used throughout the book, rather than Upper Canada or Canada West, even where these would be more accurate.

Incarnations of the Province of Ontario	
1763–1790	Province of Quebec
1791–1840	Upper Canada
1841–1867	Canada West
1867–today	Ontario

The records I focus on in the sections on students and teachers are of individual people. It is obviously not possible to list every record that falls into this category, nor, indeed, to list every repository that may hold such records, although an attempt has been made to be more inclusive in the case of the Archives of Ontario. This book is intended to act as a guide to the records that do exist and the types of institutions that should be approached when looking for these records.

The records discussed are both archival and published. In the case of the latter, in most instances the names of libraries owning each book listed are not given as has often been done in similar publications in the past. The easy access to online catalogues has made this information unnecessary. The exception is when a book appears online in its entirety, in the Internet Archive or elsewhere. The service provided by inter-library loan, available in every Canadian public library, means that unless a work is especially rare or fragile, you can obtain a copy for study.

Privacy is an issue with records less than one hundred years old and much potentially useful information is closed. For this reason, most of the discussion of archival records here ends in the early years of the twentieth century. There are exceptions, however, and with the use of published materials, such as school yearbooks, it is sometimes possible to continue a search for many years later than that. In order to have a good understanding of privacy law as it applies to family history in Ontario, it is worthwhile to have a look at Margaret Wilkinson's new book on the subject, *Genealogy and the Law in Canada.*

This book is not a general history of Ontario education. There is so much good, easily accessible information available on how education developed in the province that I did not feel that another detailed discussion of this was necessary. Many of the books and articles that are most useful for outlining the story of Ontario education are mentioned throughout this guide and in the section called Additional Works Consulted. Because there is so much information that is useful to the genealogist and the historian in these more general works, each section of this guide includes a Further Reading feature. Much of this material was selected because it not only provides a broader survey of the educational topic under discussion, but also includes names, photographs, and sources.

I enjoyed learning more about the records that exist for Ontario education as I collected material for this book. The biggest revelation has been the enormous amount of often unrecognized resources available in local archives and public libraries. So, this introduction must conclude with a thank you to all the archivists, librarians, and others who have preserved these records over the years. Without them, any exploration of the lives of teachers and students in the past would not be as rewarding as most researchers will find it to be.

CHAPTER I

Where the Resources Reside

The Archives of Ontario (AO)
134 Ian Macdonald Boulevard
Toronto, ON M7A 2C5
www.archives.gov.on.ca

The primary repository for the records of Ontario education is
the Archives of Ontario. The AO holds the records for the official bodies overseeing education in Ontario, principally in RG 2.
RG stands for "record group," which is "a body of organization-
ally related records created or collected by the same individual or
agency as part of its functions or activities." (Archives Association
of British Columbia. Glossary of Archival Terms. *aabc.ca/msa/
appendix_glossary_of_terms.htm.*)

In Canada, the term *fonds* is now typically used to describe
a record group or a manuscript group. However, in the AO context, RG is used to designate Ontario government records. For
further information on archival records and their arrangement,
see Carolynn Bart-Riedstra's book *Archives for Genealogists: A
Beginner's Guide.* (Toronto: Archives Association of Ontario and
the Ontario Genealogical Society, 2009.)

The *Archives Descriptive Database*, a searchable online guide to the holdings of the archives, can be accessed on their website. Many of the individual records available are listed and described in this book, but my emphasis is on listing those records that are likely to contain the names of individuals. Searching the AO database may uncover additional material of value to a particular research project. Not all the records listed in this book are currently described in the AO database and there are almost certainly additional sources that will emerge in the future as cataloguing continues.

The name of the department or ministry responsible for education in Ontario has changed a number of times over the years, as have the names of the subordinate agencies. The AO has a detailed outline of this history as part of the description of each record creator. Although the process of name change was not a strictly linear one, and not necessarily as straightforward as the outline below, in broad outline, education and schools were administered as follows:

1823–1833	the Council of King's College
1833–1842	the General Board of Education for Upper Canada
1842–1846	the Education Office
1846–1850	the General Board of Education for Canada West
1850–1876	the Ontario Department of Public Instruction
1876–1972	the Ontario Department of Education

Some of the materials relevant to education have been microfilmed and are readily available for inspection; some are even available for inter-library loan. Records that have not been microfilmed may be available immediately for examination, but more often will have to be retrieved from off-site.

It is necessary to be aware, when looking for details on individuals in the AO, that this information is covered by the provisions of the Freedom of Information and Protection of Privacy Act. The "freedom" part of the act means that most government information in the archives is available to you, but the "privacy" section covers, among other things, information on educational history. If the individual you are researching has been dead for a period of thirty years or more, you may access information on this person.

If the series of records you want to examine state that there are restrictions on access because the records are one hundred years old or less, you must make a request in writing to the Freedom and Privacy Unit with a five-dollar application fee. If you are visiting the AO in person, you can make an immediate request. The aim of the archives is to respond to any request for information within thirty days, although this time frame cannot always be adhered to. For more information, Customer Service Guide 109, online on the AO website, gives full details on "Freedom of Information and the Protection of Privacy."

Roy Reynolds has produced an extremely useful, although now somewhat outdated, series of guides to the educational records in the AO that are well worth reviewing. He provides a breakdown of the content of many of the records, often in much more detail than on the AO website. This series on educational records has become even more important recently, as the AO has removed the printed education-finding aid from its reading room and this series lists some materials not yet in the AO's descriptive database.

Reynolds, Roy. *Analysis of Record Group 2, Ontario Archives series C-6-C, 1865.* Toronto: Ontario Institute for Studies in Education, *circa* 1972.

——. *A Guide to Educational Materials in Municipal Records, Records of Committees and Commissions and Other Miscellaneous Papers in the Ontario Archives.* Educational Record Series no. 8. Toronto: Ontario Institute for Studies in Education, 1976.

——. *A Guide to Items Relating to Education in Papers of the Prime Minister's Department (Record Group 3) in the Ontario Archives.* Educational Record Series no. 6. Toronto: Ontario Institute for Studies in Education, 1974.

——. *A Guide to Items Relating to Education in Newspapers in the Ontario Archives.* Archives Series no. 3. Toronto: Ontario Institute for Studies in Education, *circa* 1972.

——. *A Guide to Pamphlets in the Ontario Archives Relating to Educational History, 1803–1967.* Archives Series no. 1. Toronto: Ontario Institute for Studies in Education, 1972.

——. *A Guide to Periodicals and Books Relating to Education in the Ontario Archives.* Educational Record Series no.7. Toronto: Ontario Institute for Studies in Education, 1976.

——. *A Guide to Sources in Educational History from the Private Manuscripts Section of the Archives of Ontario.* Educational Record Series no. 5. Toronto: Ontario Institute for Studies in Education, 1973.

The AO's Visual Database, available on their website, allows a search of images that relate to all things educational, using subject terms such as "school children," "schools," "scholars," "teachers," and "teachers' colleges." Images found using this method are available to order.

The Ontario Institute for Studies in Education, University of Toronto (OISE)
252 Bloor Street West

Toronto, ON M5S 1V6
www.library.utoronto.ca/oise

The OISE Library's Ontario Historical Education Collection (OHEC) is a comprehensive collection of published documents from the Ontario Ministry of Education and its predecessors. Non-governmental education materials, such as Ontario teachers' college yearbooks, are also represented. Within OHEC is the Ontario Textbook Collection (OTC), a complete collection of elementary and secondary textbooks authorized or approved for use in Ontario *circa* 1846 to 1970. Also included are some materials used in nineteenth-century schools but not approved by the Department of Education. The OHEC is open to the public by appointment. Most of the books and documents in the OHEC and OTC collections are searchable in the library's online catalogue. In addition, OISE has tried to collect class photographs and other memorabilia from the Ontario College of Education and its successors at the University of Toronto.

The broader OISE library collection contains almost all of the books and journals that have been published on Ontario education — a major part of its collection mandate.

Library and Archives Canada (LAC)
395 Wellington Street
Ottawa, ON K1A 0N4
www.collectionscanada.gc.ca

Education has been a provincial responsibility in Canada from the beginning, with the result that LAC is not a primary source of records — archival records, at least. But this does not mean there are no archival records there at all for Ontario. There is, for example, a good selection of School Daily Registers for the Sault Ste.

Marie District from the late nineteenth century to the 1930s. For the serious researcher, fonds such as B 11 — Upper Canada and Canada West: Civil Secretary, Records Relating to Education, has selected correspondence, reports, petitions, lists, returns, and other records relating to education accumulated in the Civil Secretary's Office, 1797–1843 and 1850. Also, LAC, as the national library of Canada, receives and keeps copies of all books published in this country, making it a wonderful source of school histories, teachers' memoirs, and other published works about Ontario education. (Although, it should be noted that a number of the school histories listed later in this guide are not in the LAC catalogue, presumably because the local printers and publishers involved were not aware of the depository requirements.)

The LAC website also hosts "A Virtual Schoolhouse," a digital presentation on how students in Canada experienced education one hundred years ago *(www.collectionscanada.gc.ca/schoolhouse)*.

Boards of Education Archives

Major repositories for the records of both Ontario school boards and individual schools are the archives of the various boards of education themselves. The Educational Record Series, published by OISE some thirty years ago, is still worth examining for the snapshot provided of the holdings of school boards throughout the province at one point in time.

The researchers visited each repository and catalogued what was available in considerable detail. Any school registers are noted, along with teachers' pay sheets, pupil fee books, examination records, and much more. The authors also make notes such as: "The historical records of the board are scattered and completely unsorted and un-catalogued…. Other records remain in the individual schools of the system." Fortunately, many boards have now established a centralized archive where historical material is being housed and preserved.

The Educational Record Series consists of the following:

Brett, Mark. *A Guide to Educational Records in the Possession of County Boards of Education — Northern Ontario.* Educational Record Series no. 9. Toronto: Ontario Institute for Studies in Education, 1974.

Brett, Mark, and Jack Gillespie. *A Guide to Educational Records in the Possession of County Boards of Education — South Western Ontario.* Educational Record Series no. 11. Toronto: Ontario Institute for Studies in Education, 1974.

Gillespie, Jack. *A Guide to Educational Records in the Possession of County Boards of Education — Eastern Ontario.* Educational Record Series no. 10. Toronto: Ontario Institute for Studies in Education, 1972.

Jackson, Edward. *A Guide to Educational Records in the Possession of Four City Boards of Education — Hamilton, London, Ottawa, Windsor.* Educational Record Series no. 12. Toronto: Ontario Institute for Studies in Education, 1978.

Reynolds, Roy. *An Annotated Guide to the Manuscripts in the Historical Collection of the Toronto Board of Education.* Educational Record Series no. 13. Toronto: Published by the Toronto Board of Education, in co-operation with the Department of History and Philosophy, Ontario Institute for Studies in Education, 1977.

There has been a major amalgamation of school boards since the publication of this series, to the extent that many school boards names have changed significantly. To find the current name and contact information for an Ontario school board, the Canadian Education Association's annual *KI-ES-KI Handbook: Directory of*

Key Contacts in Canadian Education can be consulted, in the section titled "School Authorities." The School Board Finder is also available on the Ontario Ministry of Education website *(www.edu. gov.on.ca/eng/sbinfo)*.

Local Archives, Historical Societies, Museums, and Public Libraries

Some school boards have transferred their historical records to the local county archive, museum, or public library. These institutions may also have their own collections of education resources built up over the years.

The Wellington County Museum and Archives has, to showcase just one example, the Attendance Register for S.S. #12 Union School, Arthur Twp. and West Luther Twp for 1891; the register for Cull's School, S.S. #2, West Garafraxa, 1930–1934; the Elora Public School daily attendance register, 1883, 1888; the Erin Village school census register, 1910–1941; the register for 1916 for S.S. #13, Maryborough Twp.; and the register for S.S. #5, Nichol Twp., 1923–1924.

Many archives and libraries also maintain an image database for their region, where photographs and postcards of schools and students usually appear. The Guelph Public Library Archives Image Database *(www.library.guelph.on.ca)* is one such database, with a wide selection of images of historic schools and their students, teachers, and administrators.

University Archives

The archives of the Ontario universities should not be discounted as a source for historical education information beyond the records of their own student body. Some have a special interest in the local history of their region and collect accordingly. The J.J. Talman Regional Collection, University of Western Ontario *(www.lib.uwo.ca/archives/talman.shtml)*, has source material on many aspects of the history and development of London, Middlesex County, and surrounding counties in southwestern Ontario. This material includes the Minutes of the London Board of Education, 1848 to1922. Brock University Archives has RG 12, a fonds that consists of daily school registers for School Section Number 2 Public School, Jordan Station, Ontario, in Louth Township, Lincoln County, 1879 to1895. Queen's University Archives *(archives.queensu.ca)* has the Kingston Board of Education fonds, with material covering 1824 to 1926, and the Midland District School Society fonds, containing records from 1818 to 1972.

Church Archives

Church archives may also have material relevant to education. Many of the early private schools and universities had church affiliations and will have records of students and teachers as a result. Although Sunday Schools are not being considered in this guide, these schools did provide education of a kind and the relevant records may be found in the denominational church archives. You can find a list of religious archives on the LAC's website *(www.collectionscanada.gc.ca/genealogy/022-806-e.html)*.

SEARCHING FOR ARCHIVAL RECORDS

Individual archives and libraries should be approached to identify what they own, but you may find useful resources on one of the federated search sites that are beginning to bring this material together in one place:

ARCHEION: Ontario's Archival Information Network

archeion-aao.fis.utoronto.ca

ARCHEION is an online search tool that provides access to descriptions of the archival records located in archives across Ontario. This is an excellent resource for finding local county archives and other archives that may hold education materials. Some school board archives are also listed.

ArchivesCanada.ca: Canadian Archival Information Network

www.archivescanada.ca

This is an archives portal maintained by the Canadian Council of Archives. From here you can search archival holdings across Canada.

OurOntario.ca

www.ourontario.ca

OurOntario is a digital partnership of many cultural and heritage organizations, archives, and libraries. It is a steadily growing site that should be searched for archival records, pamphlets, and other ephemera, and images of early Ontario schools and students.

Ontario Heritage: A Guide to Archival Resources. Cheltenham, ON: Boston Mills Press for the Toronto Area Archivists Group, 1978–80.

These guides list a number of school registers, board minutes, fee books, and other documents and photographs illustrating local school histories. The complete series was never published: Volume 1 — *Peterborough Region*; Volume 4 — *Kingston and Frontenac County*; Volume 7 — *Peel Region*; Volume 13 — *North-East Ontario.*

PUBLIC LIBRARIES

The names and contact information for many Ontario public libraries can be found on Libdex, the worldwide directory of libraries *(www.libdex.com/country/canada/ontario)*. If the library you want is not listed here, using an Internet search engine, such as Google, and the phrase "public library" followed by the name of a town or region will probably provide the necessary information to contact a local library. A new and effective resource for tracking down information in an Ontario library is AskON *(askon.ca)*, a service that delivers a real-time, collaborative virtual reference service for the province.

THE INTERNET AND ONTARIO EDUCATION

Despite what many would like to believe, not all historical records are available online, nor are they likely ever to be. But the Internet has made the search for historical sources in all areas much easier to accomplish and this proves true for educational information. Some sources, particularly out-of-copyright published books, are digitally available on the web and may be downloaded and saved on one's own computer.

The Internet Archive
www.archive.org/details/texts
Throughout this book you will find reference to websites and online documents that provide valuable information on teachers, pupils, and schools in Ontario's history. But one website stands out — the Internet Archive, particularly the section where the full text of out-of-copyright books is housed. They have, at the time of writing, 200,000 Canadian digitized books available. A

number of Ontario libraries have taken part in this project to make historical texts freely accessible. One of the leading partners in this project is the University of Toronto, and the OISE Library has made a major effort to ensure that its collection of published education documents, curricula, and textbooks have been digitized and included.

The only caveat with this site is the confusing way in which periodical literature is described and arranged. It is not easy to identify which issues of a serial publication are included and they do not appear in any organized way. It is hoped that a later version of the site will improve the periodical display.

Our Roots/Nos Racines: Canada's Local Histories Online

www.ourroots.ca

Our Roots is a steadily growing compilation of full-text books on Canadian local history. Local histories almost always include a section on a district's schools and should be searched accordingly. This site defines any book specifically on the history of a local school or schools as being within their digitization mandate and browsing through the section on the subject "Education — Ontario" will reveal many of these.

Early Canadiana Online (ECO)

www.canadiana.org/ECO

ECO is a growing digital library of Canada's print heritage from the time of the first European settlers to the first two decades of the twentieth century. The pilot project portion of ECO, which digitized 550,000 pages from the microfiche collection of the Canadian Institute for Historical Microreproduction (CIHM), and some later special projects are available as a public access collection. To search the entire collection it is necessary to visit a public or academic library that has a subscription. The freely available "Early Official Publications" has digitized many relevant education bills; the rest of ECO contains an eclectic mixture of materials relevant to Ontario education.

Canadian Institute for Historical Microreproductions (CIHM)

ECO's history extends back to 1978 when CIHM was established to locate early printed Canadian materials (books, annuals, and periodicals) so as to preserve their content in microform and to make the resulting collections available to libraries and archives. These microfiche are a treasure trove for those researching education in Ontario. Unfortunately, ECO has removed the searchable database for the microfiche from its website, but there are still two methods for searching CIHM content. The first is to find a Canadian library that owns the microfiche and to search its catalogue *(www.canadiana.org/en/co/microfiche/libraries)*; the second is to search AMICUS, Library and Archives Canada's online catalogue *(amicus.collectionscanada.gc.ca/aaweb/aalogine.htm)*. When a publication mentioned in this guide is available as a CIHM microfiche, the CIHM identifying number is given.

The types of materials chiefly available as part of CIHM are items of ephemera, which include prospectuses for early schools and school histories. Two such examples are:

Terms at Mrs. & the Miss Radcliffe's School, Niagara: Boarding with Ordinary Tuition ... 1828. CIHM microfiche series, no. 40806.

Terms of the Royal Grammar School: Established at York, Upper Canada, under the Immediate Patronage of His Excellency, the Lieutenant Governor. 1829. CIHM microfiche series, no. 40797.

THE HIDDEN INTERNET

It is important to be aware that the majority of the records that will be relevant for genealogical research in education are part of the "hidden" or "deep" Internet, where the contents of archival databases and library catalogues reside. For the searcher this means that it is necessary to go beyond the general Internet search tools, such as Google, which cannot or will not search these databases for you. If you want to find the relevant records that a library or archives might own, you must find and visit each institution's website and search whatever databases they have made available online.

NEWSPAPERS

Miss McCarty is teaching in the place of Miss Ryan who is sick with inflammation of the lungs. *Bolton Enterprise*, May 26, 1899. Quoted in Murray Hesp, *The School on the Hill: Known as Caledon East School*. (Caledon East, ON: Caledon East School Reunion Committee, 2006).

Newspapers are an invaluable source of information on teachers and schools. For the very early days of Ontario schooling often the only indication that a school existed in a community is the advertisements placed in newspapers by teachers looking for pupils. In later years, lists of school prize winners and Ontario Scholars, examination results, accounts of school events and school reunions, and many other details on schools, teachers, and scholars, both good and bad, can be found within the pages of newspapers.

To find the name of a local newspaper, consult J. Brian Gilchrist's *Inventory of Ontario Newspapers, 1793–1986.* Local public libraries and archives may have copies of early newspapers. However, many Ontario newspapers have been microfilmed and Library and Archives Canada maintains a list of *Canadian Newspapers on Microfilm Held by Libraries and Archives Canada* (*www.collectionscanada.gc.ca/8/18*). Follow the link to "Ontario" to ascertain what is available. These microfilm copies are available for inter-library loan.

Unfortunately, not many Ontario newspapers have yet been digitized and made available online. Three that have been are the *Globe and Mail* (and its predecessors) under the title *Canada's Heritage* from 1844, the *Toronto Star,* from 1894, under the title Pages of the Past (*pagesofthepast.ca*), and the *Ottawa Citizen,* which forms part of the Google News Archive Search (*news.google.ca/archivesearch*). The latter is searchable free of charge, and you should check your local public library for possible access to the other two, or visit your nearest academic library. Pages of the Past also offers personal subscriptions.

ALMANACS AND DIRECTORIES

Early almanacs and directories often listed not only schools of various types, but also the teaching staff. Toronto, in particular, is rich in early directories, and there are many other regional, county, and municipal business directories available. The series of directories that follow each have an extensive "education" section listing schools and teachers.

Scobie & Balfour's Canadian Almanac and Repository of Useful Knowledge.... (Title and publisher varies: *Scobie & Balfour's*

Canadian Almanac, 1848–50; *Scobie's Canadian Almanac,* 1851–1854; *Maclear & Co's Canadian Almanac,* 1855–1856; *Canadian Almanac and Miscellaneous Directory,* 1895–1926; *Canadian Almanac and Legal and Court Directory,* 1927–1947.) Toronto: 1848–present. Various years from 1848 to 1900 are available on the Internet Archive.

A useful source for finding relevant directories is Patricia L. Fleming's article, "A Bibliography of Ontario Directories to 1867," from *Ontario Library Review* 59 (June 1975), pages 98–107.

CENSUS RECORDS

The last few years have seen the arrival of the ability to search Ontario census records online using keywords as access points. This turns out to be a rough kind of searching, workable only for the later censuses. The word *teacher* and a location provides results if you are looking to see who was a teacher in a particular place at a particular time. This keyword search works principally when there is a group of teachers living together, such as in a convent school or a boarding school and "teacher" is used as a way of defining their relationship.

The search also identifies a teacher when he or she is a lodger and *teacher* is the word used in the relationship column. As teachers often worked away from home and boarded with local families, this applies to many in this occupation. In the 1901 census, the occupation column is also searchable for the keyword *teacher.* In 1911, using the census records provided by Ancestry.ca (*www. ancestry.ca*), approximately 350 Ontario teachers can be identified in this way. Similarly, a search can be made using the keyword *pupil* or *student* for students of boarding and residential schools.

PASSENGER LISTS

Passenger lists do not generally immediately spring to mind as a source of records on education. But now that so many are more easily accessible online with the complete image attached, it is possible to view the occupation of passengers as stated on each ship's list. An ancestor on his or her way to Canada may have listed their occupation as "teacher," which can open a new horizon for searching — in the extensive lists available for practising teachers in Ontario.

HISTORICAL PUBLISHED SOURCES

Annual Reports of the Minister of Education

Beginning in 1845/46 and first known as the *Annual Report of Common Schools in Upper Canada*, a yearly report has been made on all aspects of education in the province. It is very much worthwhile to look through the annual reports for the years of research interest as there is considerable detail on the schools and teachers of the province and many instances where individual names are listed. For example, the names of those who received provincial teaching certificates; lists of "The Superannuated or Disabled Public School Teachers," giving the teacher's name, age, years of teaching in Ontario, amount of pension, and cash paid to the pensioner that year; names of the staff of Model and Normal Schools; lists of principals and assistants of collegiate institutes and high school; and lists of school inspectors all appear throughout the years. Photographs and lists of pupils also feature, for example, in the annual reports of The Institution for the Education of the Blind. Descriptions, drawings and photographs of new schools are also frequently found.

Orders in Council (notices of administrative decisions) that related to education were sometimes included in the Annual Reports and names were often mentioned in this context. For example: John C. Reed's Public School Teacher's Certificate Cancelled (4 November 1891) and Miss M.E. Butterworth appointed first female teacher in the Girls' Model School, Ottawa, and Miss A.G. Hanahoe appointed one of the teachers in the same school. (Approved 21 March 1902).

The amount of detail and number of names varies throughout the years, with most useful information for a genealogist typically appearing in the appendices attached to each report. Much of the information elsewhere is statistical in nature, but this is frequently interesting in itself. Generally speaking, the details Annual Reports provide decrease gradually after 1900.

The Works of John George Hodgins

Hodgins, J. George, ed. *Documentary History of Education in Upper Canada, 1791–1876*, 28 volumes (Toronto: King's Printer, 1894–1910).

This twenty-eight volume documentary history is an indispensable source for anyone interested in education in Ontario. Hodgins transcribed many original documents, abstracted local histories when discussions of early schools appear, and reproduced historical statistics. His correspondence with education officials, local historians and others is summarized. He named many teachers, along with school board members and government officials. Internet Archive CIHM microfiche series, nos. 49794–822.

Hodgins, J. George, ed. *Historical and Other Papers and Documents Illustrative of the Educational System of Ontario, 1792–[1876],*

Forming an Appendix to the Annual Report of the Minister of Education. Toronto: Cameron, 1911–1912.

————. *Historical Educational Papers and Documents of Ontario.* 6 vols. Toronto: King's Printer, 1911.

————. *School Manual: The Consolidated Acts Relating to Common Schools in Upper Canada.* Toronto: Lovell and Gibson, 1861.

————. *Schools and Colleges in Ontario, 1792–1910.* Three volumes. Toronto: King's Printer, 1910.

Ryerson, Egerton. *"The Story of My Life": Being Reminiscences of Sixty Years' Public Service in Canada.* Edited by J. George Hodgins. Toronto: W. Briggs, 1883. Internet Archive.

JOHN GEORGE HODGINS, HISTORIOGRAPHER EXTRAORDINAIRE

The study of the history of Ontario education would be substantially more difficult without the work of John George Hodgins. Hodgins was born in Dublin, Ireland, in 1821 and immigrated to Upper Canada in 1832 with an uncle. While he was a student at Victoria College in Cobourg he came to the notice of its principal, Egerton Ryerson. When Ryerson became superintendent of schools in 1844, he appointed Hodgins as his clerk and later sent him to Ireland to investigate the education system there. Hodgins remained in Dublin for a year and took the course of instruction for teachers offered at the Dublin Normal School. He served as chief clerk in the education office from 1846 to 1855. He was then appointed deputy superintendent, where his loyalty, strong organizational skills, and energy allowed Ryerson to leave him in charge of practical matters so that he himself could concentrate on policy and political networking.

DOCUMENTARY HISTORY

OF

EDUCATION IN UPPER CANADA

FROM THE PASSING OF THE

CONSTITUTIONAL ACT OF 1791

TO THE

CLOSE OF THE REVEREND DOCTOR RYERSON'S ADMINISTRATION
OF THE EDUCATION DEPARTMENT
IN 1876.

VOL. IV : 1841-1843.

Edited, under the direction of the Honourable the Minister of Education, with Explanatory Notes,

BY

J. GEORGE HODGINS, M.A., LL.D., F.R.G.S.,

BARRISTER-AT-LAW,

LIBRARIAN AND HISTORIOGRAPHER TO THE EDUCATION DEPARTMENT OF ONTARIO.

TORONTO:

WARWICK BRO'S & RUTTER, PRINTERS, &C., &C., 68 AND 70 FRONT STREET WEST.
1897.

The title page of one volume of J. George Hodgins's multi-volume documentary history of Ontario education.

After Ryerson retired in 1876, Hodgins's relationship with the two subsequent ministers of education did not provide him with the same autonomy and responsibility and he reluctantly resigned in 1890 from the position of deputy minister. He retained the position of librarian until 1904, and until his death in 1912 he held the post of historiographer.

Hodgins is most remembered for his immense output of reports, articles, speeches, pamphlets, and textbooks. In this position as historiographer, he collected and published a vast array of original documents pertaining to public and private education in Ontario. Much of what he gathered came from direct appeals he made to teachers to tell him of their early experiences. His twenty-eight-volume *Documentary History of Education in Upper Canada, 1791–1876* gives an unparalleled, although somewhat slanted, view of the development of schooling in the province. He was also responsible for compiling the Annual Reports of the Department of Public Instruction and its successor authorities until he left the post of deputy minister. These reports also greatly add to our knowledge of Ontario education.

He had a more direct effect on schooling with the textbooks he produced on geography and on the history of Canada, which were authorized for use in the schools for a number of years.

Sadly, there has never been a full-length biography of this man with the prodigious work ethic, although he does have an entry in the *Dictionary of Canadian Biography (www.biographi.ca)*.

Journals

The education journals published in the nineteenth century are not particularly useful for finding lists of names, but they do offer an unparalleled view of the concerns of early educators in Ontario:

Canada Educational Monthly. Toronto: Canada Educational Monthly Publishing Company, 1879–1905. Internet Archive — selected issues.

Canada School Journal. Toronto: Canada School Journal Publishing Co., 1877–1887.

The Canadian Teacher. Toronto: Educational Publishing Co., 1897– *circa* 1981. Formed by the union of the *Canada School Journal* and the *Educational Weekly.*

Educational Journal. Toronto: Educational Publishing Co., 1887– 1897. A merger of the *Canada School Journal* and the *Educational Weekly.*

Educational Weekly. Toronto: Grip Printing and Publishing, 1885– 1887.

Journal of Education for Upper Canada. Toronto: J.H. Lawrence, 1848–1877. Internet Archive — selected issues.

Ontario Teacher. Strathroy, ON: Ross & McColl for the Council of Public Instruction, 1873–1876.

School. Toronto: Ontario College of Education, University of Toronto, 1912–1946.

Contemporary Published Sources

Fleming, William Gerald. *Ontario's Educative Society.* Seven volumes. Toronto: University of Toronto Press, 1971–1972. Volume 1: *The Expansion of the Educational System.* Volume 2: *The Administrative Structure.* Volume 3: *Schools, Pupils, and Teachers.* Volume 4: *Post-Secondary and Adult Education.* Volume 5: *Supporting Institutions and Services.* Volume 6: *Significant Developments in Local School Systems.* Volume 7: *Educational Contributions of Associations.*

Harris, Robin S. *An Index to the Material Bearing on Higher Education Contained in J.G. Hodgins' Documentary History of Education in Upper Canada (Ontario).* Toronto: Innis College, University of Toronto, 1966.

Reynolds, Roy. *A Guide to Published Government Documents Relating to Education in Ontario.* Archives Series no. 2. Toronto: Ontario Institute for Studies in Education, 1972.

CHAPTER 2

Students in Ontario Schools

The early European immigrants to the infant Upper Canada came for many reasons — fleeing the Revolutionary War to the south, as economic migrants hoping to escape low wages and unemployment, or, for those with more resources, in search of adventure and independence. What they had in common was the need to make a living in a cash-poor society, whether by establishing a farm on uncleared land, a small business in one of the new towns or settlements springing up, or by hiring out their services as farm or house servants to others who needed them.

The labour of children and young adults was a vital part of all these enterprises and there was no time for extended periods of schooling, even if there had been the schools available. As Susan Houston and Alison Prentice point out in *Schooling and Scholars in Nineteenth Century Ontario*, "It was not in schools and colleges that the vast majority of Upper Canadian boys and girls learned the skills that they would need to function as adults."

The basics of reading and writing were frequently passed along to children by their mothers and fathers or by other adults in the community who had the time to spare. The letters of Anne Langton, who writes in 1837 about life on Sturgeon Lake in the

Newcastle District, refer throughout to the informal schooling she offered to her neighbours' children:

> I had Menzies' two little girls for a lesson today. I have lately begun to teach them a little. They come for about an hour three times a week; as yet we are not all perfect in our letters, and I sometimes feel that, unaccustomed as I am to teaching, I shall not accomplish much in my short schooling. But one good effect it appears to have, that they get a little more teaching at home.
>
> I had a new pupil today, a little girl of the Daniels about ten years old. I scarcely yet know what her attainments are, for she is dreadfully frightened, and though she appeared to know scarcely more than her letters at first, I shall not think it all my own doing if I find that she can read at the end of a fortnight. I hope she will get some good from me, however, for she has nearly two miles to come for her lesson.

Langton's letters continue to chronicle the beginning of formalized schooling in her locality, which mirrors the activity elsewhere in the province. In 1841, with a small legacy, she purchased land to donate for a school as neighbours have agreed to help with the building and there are sufficient children in the neighbourhood to qualify for the government grant of £10 per year to support a teacher.

John Graves Simcoe, Upper Canada's initial lieutenant-governor from 1791 to 1796, was the first to see the need for schooling in the colony, even if he only recognized it as being necessary for the children of the elite. His plans were never realized, but in 1797 a request was made to set aside five hundred thousand acres of crown land as reserves to support grammar schools and a university at some time in the future. The lands were set aside, but it would be many years until the proceeds would be used to support education in the province.

In 1807, legislation was passed to establish grammar schools, (originally intended to provide a classical education for older students), followed in 1816 by the first of the Common School Acts. Common schools — the word *common* refers to the fact that they were intended to educate children of all social classes and religions — were to provide what we would now call an elementary education. A series of acts to refine the initial legislation followed, until 1855, when Egerton Ryerson, the first Superintendent of Education, felt able to announce that the basic structure of the provincial school system was complete. It was, of course, to be many more years before universal schooling in a form that we would recognize today was finally achieved.

The Common School Act of 1816 set aside a grant of £6,000 to be divided among the then nine administrative districts — Western, London, Niagara, Home, Newcastle, Hamilton, Midland, Johnstown, and Eastern — for the establishment of the said common schools. Locally elected school trustees could receive a share of this grant if they were to provide a schoolhouse and part of a teacher's salary, on the condition that there were at least twenty pupils available to attend.

The Common School Act of 1841 created district school boards and a Superintendent of Common Schools, and established local property assessment to help support the schools. In addition, in a move that would eventually prove of value to historical researchers, this act set out the requirement for the completion of forms reporting on educational activities in the districts. A succession of educational acts followed throughout the century, refining and expanding the legislation relating to the common schools.

Before the 1850s, secondary education as we would recognize it today did not exist. To a large extent, boys and girls were educated separately at institutions run by the church or by private individuals. The curriculum was not divided into what was distinctly an elementary and a secondary level and indeed the terms, elementary, secondary, and high school were still being defined and what was meant by each in Ontario was slowly being established. Secondary education as we understand it today — as the second section of a three-part progression from elementary school to a post-secondary institution — was not in place until the 1880s.

GRAMMAR SCHOOLS

In 1807 the District Schools Act made provision for £100 to be provided for the salary of one grammar school teacher in each of the eight administrative districts. Trustees were appointed for each school with the duties of hiring the teacher and drafting the necessary rules and regulations. No provision, however, was made for a school building and all operating expenses apart from the teacher's salary had to be found by other means, such as school fees. As the number of administrative districts grew, so did the number of grammar schools, until there were thirteen in 1839.

In 1839 the £100 grant was confirmed, but funds were allocated from the School Reserves, established in 1798, to build school buildings and to establish grammar schools outside the principal towns of each district. Increasingly thereafter towns and villages sought to persuade politicians to provide their area with a school, which led to a huge leap in the numbers. As the money provided was inadequate for the number of schools and administrative oversight was minimal, the quality of education provided by each school varied widely depending on where the school was located, the quality of the teachers, and who chose to send their children.

The original idea of a grammar school was one where the classics were taught, but this distinction had waned by the middle of the century with some grammar schools no longer providing an education in the classics and some common schools doing so. In addition, by 1855, a large number of girls were attending the grammar schools; by 1870, 90 percent had some female pupils.

PUBLIC SCHOOLS AND HIGH SCHOOLS

The Schools Improvement Act of 1871 changed the name of the common schools to public schools, and grammar schools to high schools. With this act, for the first time education became compulsory with all children required to attend schools from the age of seven to twelve. High-school education was formally extended to both boys and girls and the education offered would be in English and scientific studies, rather than in the classics. Those schools that were able to meet special conditions — a minimum number of teachers and male pupils studying the classics — and who so desired could qualify for an additional grant and call themselves a "collegiate institute."

Only a few communities were ever able to qualify. The stage was now set for the public schools to become feeder schools for secondary-level education at the high-school level, with that then leading, for a small minority still at first, to study at the university level.

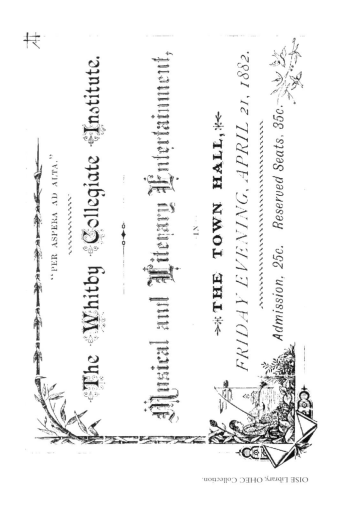

A ticket for a concert by pupils of the Whitby Collegiate Institute.

41

Further Reading

Bell, Walter. *The Development of the Ontario High School.* Toronto: University of Toronto Press, 1918.

Gidney, R.D. *Inventing Secondary Education: The Rise of the High School in Nineteenth-Century Ontario.* Montreal: McGill-Queen's University Press, 1990.

Houston, Susan E., and Alison Prentice. *Schooling and Scholars in Nineteenth-Century Ontario.* Toronto: University of Toronto Press, 1988.

LISTS OF STUDENTS

School Registers

Although the blanket statement is often made that "almost no school registers exist," in fact a number of school registers have survived from the nineteenth century and even more from the twentieth century. Some runs of registers are remarkably complete, as is the case, for example, with the registers of Hess Street School in what is now the Hamilton–Wentworth District School Board. It is not possible here to list all those that exist; instead you should contact the relevant board of education and/or local archives and public library to find out what exists in a particular area. When searching an archival database, useful search terms include the name of a school or school district, or phrases such as "school register," "school registers," "daily registers," etc.

"An Early School Register." Lennox and Addington Historical Society, *Papers and Records* 5 (1914), 28–61. A complete reproduction of a school register, beginning in 1831. The names of the

Public (or Separate) School, in School Section No. _17_ of the Township of _Vaughan_,

in the _Villa of_ _Kleinburg_ (If there are two or more schools under the control of the Board,
(City, Town or Village.)   the local name should be inserted in the next blank.)

		PUPILS				PARENTS OR GUARDIANS			
REGISTER NUMBER	FORM	NAME	Year	Month	Day	NAME	ADDRESS	BOYS	GIRLS
1	IV	Ruby Gould	05	July	14	Jno. Gould	Kleinburg		/
2		Merle Hambly	05	Feb.	13	Arthur Hambly	Kleinburg		/
3		Beatrice Wild	03	Oct.	31	Edward Wild	..		/
4		Gordon Train	03	Sept	6	Lou. Train		/	
5		Mary Kaiser	06	Mar	10	Levi Kaiser			/
6	III.	Freda Adcock	06	July	2	Fred Adcock			/
7		Lorne Burkitt	05	Feb.	7	Samuel Burkitt		/	
8		Eldon Coward	05	Aug	29	James Coward		/	
9		Velma Hawman	05	Aug	20	Stewart Hawman			/
0	I	Saul Kaiser	16			Levi Kaiser		/	
1	II.	George Hollingshead	13	Feb.	24	Arthur Hollingshead	..	/	
2		Ada Burkitt	11	Nov.	1	Samuel Burkitt			/
3		Annie Gould	10	Mar.	2	Jno. Gould	..		/
4		Herbie Hilliard	12	Apr.	18	Samuel Hilliard		/	
5		Otto Train	12	Oct.	7	Lou. Train	..	/	
6		James Wild	12	Dec.	8	Edward Wild		/	
7		Willie Lyons	12	July	26	Arthur Colton		/	
8		Mabel Kaiser	10	Dec.	20	Levi Kaiser			/
9	II.	Willie Devins	10	Sept	12	Albert Devins		/	
0		Eric Adcock	10	Dec.	17	Fred Adcock		/	
1		Kenneth Gould	9	Oct	8	Jno. Gould		/	
2		Vera Hollingshead	10	Feb.	26	Arthur Hollingshead	..		/
3		Thelma Jones	10	Feb.	20	Chas. Jones	..		/
4		Irene Ryder	10	May	23	Joe Ryder	..		/
5		Edith Simpson	12	Nov.	10	Jos. Simpson			/
6		Ewart Hawman	10	July	15	Stewart Hawman	..	/	
7		Bertha Kershner	8						/
8	I.	Mervin Kaiser	9	July	31	Levi Kaiser		/	
9		Maggie Cairns	8	Mar.	9	J. Cairns			/
0		Maggie Boyce	10	June	30	W. Boyce			/
1		Charles Wild	8	Nov.	9	Edward Wild	..	/	
2		Nelson Burkitt	8	July	7	Samuel Burkitt	..	/	
3		Ivy Adcock	8	Jan	23	Fred Adcock	..		/
4	I(c)	Harry Burgess	6					/	
5	I(b)	Mervyn Gould	7	Oct	24	Jno. Gould		/	
6		Annie White	8	Apr		R. White			/
7		Olive Boyce	8	Dec	24	W. Boyce			/
8		Eveline Jones	6	July	21	Chas. Jones			/
9		Everett Arth	10	April	21	W. Arth	Woodbridge, R.R.	/	
0		Tommy Ryder	8	Jan	14	Jos. Ryder	Kleinburg.	/	
1		Wilma Adcock	7	Nov	4	Fred Adcock			/
2		Gordon White	6	Mar		R. White	.	/	
3		Army Hawman	10	Mar	4	S. Hawman			/
4	I(c)	Kenneth Hawman	6			S. Hawman	..	/	
5	"	Molly Adcock	5	Aug.	2	Fred Adcock.	..		/
6	I(a)	Ernest Ryder	6	Aug	10	J. Ryder		/	
7		James Kerr	10	July	7	W. Kerr		/	
8		Irene Devins	6	July	4	A. Devins.			/
9	I(c)	Mary Gould	5	Mar	14	Jno. Gould			/
0	"	Eleanor Devins	7	June		Jno. A. Devins			/

TEACHER'S NAME	ADDRESS	DATE OF APPOINTMENT
Margaret Semple	Kleinburg.	Jan 17
Ruth M. Woodger	Kleinburg	Sept. 3 18

(If there is a change of teacher during the year, use the second line.)

School Register for Kleinburg School, S.S. No. 17, 1918.

students are those of the earliest settlers of Ernesstown, east of Millhaven. Internet Archive.

AO RG 2-42 Department of Education Select Subject Files, mostly 1885–1913. RG 2-42 consists primarily of the voluminous education department incoming correspondence files. It is worth the time to find the relevant correspondence for your area as ancestors may have written letters to the Minister of Education, signed petitions as taxpayers in favour of a new school being established, or served as school trustees. Available on microfilm.

Tucked away in the correspondence can also be found the occasional school register. For example:

AO RG 2-42-0-5803 Parry Sound Lumber Company Camp Schools #2 and #3. Daily registers for 1909.

AO RG 2-42-0-6500 Tilbury North Township, S.S. #2 (Stoney Point). Establishment of Separate School. Includes list of pupils (attendance register) for 1901.

Barnett, John. "An Early Red School House and Its Century-Old Record Book." *Ontario History* 48, no. 1 (1956), 7–17. This article refers to an early school in S.S. No. 5, Toronto Township, colloquially known as the Red School House. Unfortunately, although the author refers to his being about to donate the register to the provincial archives, the Archives of Ontario does not have in its possession.

Ontario Student Records (OSRs)

The Ontario Student Record or OSR is the record of a student's educational progress through schools in Ontario. Established first in 1950 as a voluntary system and known as the Ontario School Record, in 1973 it became officially the Ontario Student Record, an ongoing record that is transferred from school to school.

Privacy legislation does not allow the OSRs to be examined by anyone other than the person to whom the information relates, or the student's parents until he or she reaches eighteen. Part of the content of the OSR must be retained for fifty-five years after the student leaves the Ontario school system. All this effectively means that this potentially invaluable source is not available to researchers. For the full details on OSRs, see Ontario Student Record (OSR) Guideline 2000, at *www.edu.gov.on.ca/ eng/document/curricul/osr/osr.html*.

Other Lists

Some of the earliest lists of students are found in official records. *A Guide to Published Government Documents Relating to Education in Ontario* gives a detailed outline of the information on teachers and pupils contained in the *Appendices to the Journals of the Legislative Assembly of Upper Canada*, 1825–1840. Most importantly, these appendices printed the (not always complete) District Grammar and Common School Reports. The Grammar School Reports sometimes contained the names of pupils, for example, as in the Western District and Midland District Reports for 1829.

Lennox, Donald H. "The Strachan Lists." *Families* 33, no. 3 (1994), 143–49. Reproduces three appendices of students whom John Strachan taught or admitted into the church, one of which is an "Alphabetical List of 'Young Gentlemen' Now Living (i.e. 26 November 1827) Who Have Been Educated by the Honourable and Right Reverend John Strachan, D.D., Archdeacon of York (Now Toronto) in Upper Canada."

Booth, Lee. "Report of a Common School in Elizabeth Township Leeds County: 1842." *Families* 15, no. 3 (1976), 78–82. A list of pupils for the school for that year.

AO RG 2-21 Grammar School Trustees Half-Yearly Returns and Annual Reports, 1854–1871. Lists of student names and ages can be found in the half-yearly returns, arranged by school. Online finding aid available.

School Yearbooks

High-school yearbooks are an extremely valuable source of student names and, in the later years, photographs of groups and individuals. Local history collections in public libraries and archives are a good source for these, as are board of education archives. It should also be noted that some schools, high schools in particular, maintain their own formal or informal archives — Humberside Collegiate in Toronto, for example, has its own professional-level archives.

Contact an individual school when you are looking for yearbooks. You may also need to consult the school (or a school history) to find out the name given to a year book. The Brampton High School's publication was known as *The Quill* and in its pages can be found such valuable lists as a 1944 honour roll and a record of all those who served in the Second World War. School yearbooks can often also be found for purchase from online auction sites such as eBay. Some schools, for example Port Credit Secondary School, have burned CDs of their yearbooks and offer them for sale.

Nineteenth-Century and Twentieth Century Yearbook Examples

Old Boys Association. *Toronto Grammar School Yearbook, (The Old Blue School) Founded in 1807, Now The Collegiate Institute, Jarvis Street.* Toronto: Bryan Press, 1897. Internet Archive.

Trent University Archives, Peterborough. Peterborough Collegiate and Vocational Institute fonds, 1905–1977. Note particularly the fifty-eight volumes of the school yearbook, *The Echoes*, and thirteen scattered volumes of "Commencement Exercises" between 1937 and 1951.

EXAMINATIONS

Draw an outline map of Ontario, marking the position of Ottawa, Pembroke, Collingwood, Kincardine, Sarnia, Port Dover, Niagara Falls. Trace a railway route from each of four of these places to Toronto.

— High School Entrance: Geography: December Examinations, 1888.

A and B begin business together; A gives 3/5 of the capital. At the end of the first year they have made a net profit of 3%; at the end of the second a net profit of 5%; at the end of the third they are bankrupts and can only pay 50 cents in the dollar. The remaining money is $21,735;

47

how much did each contribute?

— Examination Papers Suitable for
Intermediate Examination, reprinted from
School Examiner and Student's Assistant for 1881
(Toronto: W.J. Gage, 1882), 5. Internet Archive.

Department of Education, Ontario

Annual Examinations, 1922

JUNIOR PUBLIC SCHOOL GRADUATION

ENGLISH GRAMMAR

Values	
	1. While Nell *was preparing* supper, I noticed *that* her grandfather observed me *more* closely than he had done *before*. We had scarcely begun our meal when there was a knock at the door by *which* I had entered. The next *moment there appeared* a *lad* with the most comical expression of face I have ever seen.
2 × 6 = 12	(*a*) Write in full the subordinate clauses in the above extract, and give the kind and the relation of each.
2 × 9 = 18	(*b*) Parse the italicized words.
12	2. Analyse fully :—
	At last awakes the hidden breeze That bears me to the land of dreams, Where music sighs among the trees And murmurs in the winding streams.

A question from the 1922 English grammar examination for graduation from junior public school.

It was common at all levels of schooling to award book prizes to high achievers. You might find them among the family memorabilia that has been passed down through the generations. They provide important clues as to schools attended and levels of education achieved.

A provincial entrance examination to set a standard for those students wishing to attend a high school or a collegiate institute

48

was introduced in 1871. This was followed in 1876 by the Intermediate Examination to determine who progressed from the lower school (forms I and II of high school) to the upper school (forms III and IV of high school).This Intermediate Examination was so challenging and led to such criticism that it was abolished in 1882. A look at the questions asked in these examinations gives an idea of the high standards required of Ontario students.

At the end of high school, there was another hurdle — the matriculation examination.This served as an end-of-high-school rite of passage as well as an examination for university entrance.

The Examination Papers and Those Who Passed Them

The AO RG 2-133 Reports of Academic Standing/Student Records contain examination results of students who wrote the various provincial-wide examinations between 1867 and 1917. The reports document the student's name, age, where the exam was written, when it was written, and the grades the student received.This record group does not appear in the AO Archives descriptive database. The first six years have not been micro-filmed, but from 1873/74 to 1900/02 are available on microfilms, MS 7322 to MS 7369.

Local newspapers reported examination results on a regular basis and you should search for the results at all levels.

One important examination was the Examination for Admission of Students to High Schools and Collegiate Institutes. The OHEC collection has a large number of these examination papers covering various years from 1873 to 1949, when the entrance examination was abolished.The collection also includes middle school and upper school examinations, Grade 12 departmental examinations, and Grade 13 examinations.The latter were discontinued in 1967, meaning the end of province-wide exams.

Ontario examination papers are also often reproduced in the Annual Reports of the Department of Education and in various educational periodicals. They are also sometimes found published in other contexts; for example:

Ladies Seminary, Toronto, Ontario. *Programme of the Yearly Examinations in the Ladies' Seminary, Wellington Street, Toronto, July 23, 1852.* ECO CIHM microfiche series, no. 43663. The original is in the Baldwin Room of TRL.

SEPARATE SCHOOLS

Roman Catholic schools have been a part of schooling in Ontario since the very earliest years. The first recorded was a French-language school opened in Fort Frontenac (today Kingston) in 1676. In 1804 the first English-language Catholic school was established at St. Raphael's in Glengarry County.

St. Mary's Separate School, North Bay.

The move toward legislated separate religious schooling, which came during the period from 1841 to 1867 when Upper Canada was joined with Lower Canada as Canada West and Canada East respectively, was desired by both Catholics and Protestants, each group having their own motives for wanting separate, publicly supported schools. School Acts of 1841 and 1843 established the principle of separate schools in the province, a fact Egerton Ryerson, an opponent of separate schooling, had to accept when he became Superintendent of Education in 1844.

The separate school question was not initially a contentious issue, but after 1852, factors such the growing conservatism of the Catholic Church, the accompanying growth of Protestant anti-Catholicism, and the rising tide of Irish Catholic immigration all combined to make Roman Catholic separate schooling a problematic thorn in the side of Ontario education. Further acts strengthened separate schools and their funding and by the 1880s, nearly 30,000 students were educated in this way.

There are separate Roman Catholic school boards for most areas of the province, which can be located in the same way as other school boards.

Histories of Separate Schools and Schooling

Bennett, John M. "Separate Catholic Schools in Northern Ontario, Pembroke to Manitoba Boundary: Facts Obtained on Some of Them in 1921." Unpublished manuscript, n.d. A history of these schools by the Provincial Separate School Inspector for the area from 1917–1959. OHEC.

Buonocore, S.P. *Catholic Education on the Northern Frontier: The Origins and Early Development of the Port Arthur Roman*

Catholic Separate School Board, 1870–1888. Thunder Bay, ON: The Author, 1992.

Cameletti, John R. *A History of the Separate Schools of the City of Sault Ste. Marie.* Sault Ste. Marie, ON: Sault Ste. Marie Separate School Board, 1967.

Catholic Education in Cornwall, Ontario: Yesterday, Today and Tomorrow. Cornwall, ON: Stormont, Dundas, and Glengarry County Roman Catholic Separate School Board, 1971.

Corrigan, Gerry, ed. *Catholic Education in Dufferin-Peel: A Story Worth Telling.* Mississauga, ON: Dufferin-Peel Roman Catholic Separate School Board, 1988.

Dixon, Robert T. *We Remember, We Believe: A History of Toronto's Catholic Separate School Boards, 1841 to 1997.* Toronto: Toronto Catholic District School Board, 2007.

Flynn, L.J. *At School in Kingston, 1850–1973: The Story of Catholic Education in Kingston and District.* Kingston, ON: Frontenac, Lennox and Addington County Roman Catholic Separate School Board, 1973.

Mary of St. Catherine (Sister). "The Genesis of Catholic Education in Renfrew." Master's thesis, University of Ottawa, 1958.

One Hundred of Years of Catholic Education, 1884–1994: The Catholic Separate Schools of Sudbury. Sudbury, ON: Catholic Separate Schools of Sudbury, 1984.

Our Roots — Our Story: A History of Catholic Education in Huron and Perth Counties. Dublin, ON: Huron-Perth Catholic District School Board History Book Committee, 2007.

Sylvestre, Paul-Francois. *130 Years of Excellence: The Ottawa Roman Catholic Separate School Board, 1856–1986.* Ottawa, ON: The Ottawa Roman Catholic Separate School Board, 1986.

Villeneuve, Rudolph. *Catholic Education in Cornwall, Ontario: Yesterday, Today and Tomorrow.* Cornwall, ON: Stormont,

Dundas, and Glengarry County Roman Catholic Separate
School Board, 1971.

Further Reading

Hodgins, J. George. *The Legislation and History of Separate Schools
in Upper Canada, from 1841, Until the Close of the Rev. Dr.
Ryerson's Administration of the Education Department of Ontario
in 1876; Including Various Private Papers and Documents on the
Subject.* Toronto: W. Briggs, 1897. Internet Archives.
Stamp, Robert M. *The Historical Background to Separate Schools in
Ontario.* Toronto: Ontario Ministry of Education, 1985.

PRIVATE SCHOOLS

The Rev. Thomas Handcock, A.B., of Trinity
College, Dublin, Assistant Chaplain to the
force at Niagara, informs the public that he
has opened an Academy for the instruction of
youths in Greek, Latin, etc. at Butler's Barracks.

— *Niagara Gleaner* (12 August 1826).
Quoted in J. George Hodgins, *Documentary
History of Education in Upper Canada*, vol. 1
(Toronto: King's Printer, 1894), 229.

Ontario's first private schools were neither
schools of class-based privilege nor schools
of religious protest. They were, quite simply, schools of necessity. At a time in the late

eighteenth century when the state was not involved in education, families who desired schooling for their children had of necessity to turn to the private sector.

> — Robert M. Stamp, *A History of Private Schools in Ontario* (Toronto: Report commissioned for the Commission on Private Schools in Ontario, 1984), 1.

It is very difficult to know how many private schools there were in early Ontario, as most were very small — perhaps with as few as three or four pupils — and were in existence for very brief periods. Frequently begun by clergymen or perhaps widowed or single middle-class or gentlewomen, the fees they provided were often seen as a supplement to income. An example of one such "private venture" school, still in existence today, is Trinity College School in Port Hope. An Anglican clergyman, William A. Johnson, opened the school in his parsonage in 1862 in the village of Weston, with the first pupils being his own three sons.

Much of the detail that can be retrieved about these establishments comes from the advertisements for students found in early newspapers or from occasional documents found in family papers. R.D. Gidney has collected mention of 350 what he calls "voluntary" schools between 1830 and 1870 using local newspapers and Education Department statistical records, while acknowledging that his list is by no means complete.

In the cash-poor society of Ontario in the 1800s, finding the money necessary to pay school fees for education past the elementary level was a real problem for many middle-class families, whose first choice was not the grammar schools that, although also requiring fees, were open to all to attend. But it was not until public, state-funded schooling had really taken hold in Ontario in the mid- to late-nineteenth century that private, or independent schools, came to be seen as a distinctly different educational choice.

Although most private schools were small and short-lived, a number of them, usually associated with a religious denomination, did survive and are well-established today. After 1900, few new private schools had specific ties with a particular church or style of religion. The independent schools that continue to exist are proud of their long history and maintain their own historical archives. Contact information for those schools that belong to the Canadian Association of Independent Schools can be found on the association's website (*www.cais.ca/Ontario*).

Albert College, Belleville (1857)

McGregor, Alex. "Egerton Ryerson, Albert Carman, and the Founding of Albert College, Belleville." *Ontario History*, 63, no. 4 (December, 1971), 203–16.

Smith, W.E.L. *Albert College, 1857–1957*. Belleville, ON: Intelligencer Ltd., 1957.

Appleby College, Oakville

Opened as a private venture school in 1911 by John F.H. Guest with the financial assistance of his father-in-law, Sir Edmund Walker, Appleby continues as a residential school only.

Ashbury College, Ottawa

Opened in 1891 by the Anglican clergyman George Penrose Woollcombe with just nine boys, it was named Ashbury College in 1900.

Hillfield-Strathallan College, Hamilton

Hillfield College for boys was opened in 1901 as the Ontario School and then became known as Highfield. In 1920 the school became Hillcrest, and finally, in 1928, Hillfield College. An amalgamation in 1962 with Strathallan, a school for girls established in 1923, created Hillfield-Strathallan College.

Lakefield College School, Lakefield

Established in 1879 as Sparham Sheldrake's Preparatory School for Boys or The Grove, and then later named Lakefield Preparatory School.

Harris, Andrew, ed. *Lakefield College School: The First 100 Years.* Toronto: Pagurian Press, 1979.

Pickering College, Newmarket

Founded by the Quakers near Picton in 1842 as the Westlake Boarding School, it was reopened in Newmarket in 1927.

St Andrew's College, Aurora

Founded in Toronto in 1899, the school moved to its current home in 1924.

Scoular, William. *Not an Ordinary Place: A St. Andrew's Century.* Aurora, ON: St. Andrew's College, 1998.

St. Michael's College School, Toronto

Founded in 1852 by the Basilian Fathers, St. Michael's originally offered a combination of what would today be considered high-school and university education.

Students in Ontario Schools

Ridley College, St. Catharines
Opened in 1899 as a Low Church Anglican alternative to schools such as Trinity College School.

Beattie, K. *Ridley: The Story of a School*. 2 volumes. St. Catharines, ON, 1963.
A Memorial Service for Old Ridleians Who Gave Their Lives in the War: June 22, 1919. St. Catharines, ON: Ridley College, 1919.

Trinity College School, Port Hope
Founded in 1865 in Weston, Ontario, and moved to Port Hope in 1868.

Humble, A.H. *The School on the Hill: Trinity College School, 1865–1965*. Port Hope, ON: Trinity College School, 1965.
Old Boys' Association. *Trinity College School Old Boys at War: 1899–1902, 1914–1918, 1939–1945*. Port Hope, ON: Trinity College School, Old Boys' Association, 1948. Internet Archive.

Upper Canada College, Toronto
Founded in 1929, Upper Canada College is the oldest independent school in Ontario.

Dickson, George and Adam, G. Mercer. *A History of Upper Canada College, 1829–1892: With Contributions by Old Upper Canada College Boys: Lists of Head-Boys, Exhibitioners, University Scholars, and Medallists, and a Roll of the School*. Toronto: Rowsell & Hutchison, 1893. Internet Archive CIHM microfiche series, no. 02659
The Roll of Pupils of Upper Canada College, Toronto, January 1830 to June 1916. Kingston, ON: Hanson, Crozier and Edgar,

57

1917. Reprinted. Milton, ON: Global Heritage Press, 2009.

Upper Canada College. *The Upper Canada College Register Containing the Prize List and Examination Papers...* Toronto, 1840–1842.

University of Toronto Archives A1974-0018 and A1976-0003. Upper Canada College Records, 1829–1892. This record grouping includes student registers, punishment record books, parents' accounts, scholarships and bursaries, and fee books.

Bishop Strachan School, Toronto
Opened in 1867 as a school for Anglican young ladies.

AO F1119 Bishop Strachan School Collection, 1917–1942. Published materials relating to the school with information on the history and activities of the school, on staff as well as alumni birth, marriages and deaths. Available on microfilm.

Branksome Hall School, Toronto
Founded in 1903 by Margaret Scott, an experienced Ontario educator, and Florence Merrick.

Robertson, Heather. *The Road Well Kept: Branksome Hall Celebrates 100 Years.* Toronto: ECW Press, 2002.

Havergal College, Toronto
Founded in 1894 by evangelical Anglicans as a sister school to Ridley College.

Byers, Mary. *Havergal: Celebrating a Century, 1894–1994.* Toronto: Published for Havergal College by the Boston Mills Press, 1994.

St. Clement's School, Toronto

An Anglican school founded in 1901, St. Clement's was originally coeducational. The boys soon moved to form a new school, St. Clement's College, first in Toronto and later in Brampton. It closed shortly thereafter, but the girl's section of the school, still in Toronto, continued to prosper.

St. Mildred's-Lightbourn School, Oakville

Originally established in Toronto in 1891 by the Anglican religious order Seven Sisters of the Church, St. Mildred's was the first of the order's schools outside England. In the 1960s, St. Mildred's moved to Oakville and amalgamated with a private elementary school, the Lightbourn School.

Trafalgar Castle School, Whitby

Founded in 1894 as the Ontario Ladies' College, with a Methodist Church affiliation.

Ontario Ladies' College. *Vox Collegi: Centennial Edition, 1874–1974.* Whitby, ON: 1974. Includes a history of the college by Brian Winter.

Commencement Exercises of the Ontario Ladies College, Whitby, Ontario, June 12th to 17th, 1887. Oshawa Digital Archive (*localhistory.oshawalibrary.ca*).

Selected List of Other Private Schools No Longer in Existence for Which Some Resources or Information Exists

Bishop Bethune College, Oshawa

Incorporated in 1889 as a private school for girls, it closed in 1932.

Bishop Bethune College: A Church Boarding and Day School for Girls. This eighteen-page booklet outlines the staff, curriculum, regulations, and fees. Oshawa Digital Archive (*localhistory. oshawalibrary.ca*).

Burlington Ladies' Academy, Hamilton
Founded in 1845

Catalogue of the Officers and Students of the Burlington Ladies' Academy of Hamilton, Canada for the Winter Session of 1847. Hamilton, ON, 1847. CIHM microfiche series, no. 55448; ECO; AO.

F3359 Jane Van Norman fonds, United Church of Canada Archives. Correspondence, including letters re: Burlington Ladies' Academy, Hamilton, *circa* 1844–1857. Jane Van Norman was one of the founders of the Burlington Ladies' Academy.

Demill Ladies' College, Oshawa
Founded in 1876 by the Reverend Alfred Byron Demill, the school closed in 1896.

Demill Ladies' College, Commencement Exercises, June 17, 19, 20, 21, 1892. Oshawa Digital Archive (*localhistory.oshawalibrary.ca*).
Eleventh Annual Calendar of Demill Ladies' College, Oshawa, Ont: For the Collegiate Year, 1887–8. Oshawa Digital Archive (*localhistory.oshawalibrary.ca*).

Eclectic Female Institute, Brampton

Eclectic Female Institute, Brampton, C.W.: Established Sept. 1, 1861, Henry H. Hutton, A.M., Principal. Toronto: W.C. Chewett, 1863. CIHM microfiche series, no. 61752. A list of female and, interesting enough, male pupils included in what is essentially a school prospectus.

Rockwood Academy, Rockwood

Sherk, A.B. "A Pioneer Academy." *Ontario Historical Society Papers and Records* 23 (1926), 466–69.

Further Reading

Gossage, Carolyn. *A Question of Privilege: Canada's Independent Schools.* Toronto: Peter Martin, 1977.

Johnson, Dana. *For the Privileged Few: The Private and Specialist Schools of Ontario, 1800–1930.* Parks Canada Research Bulletin no. 215. Ottawa, ON: Parks Canada, 1984.

Stamp, Robert M. *A History of Private Schools in Ontario.* Toronto: Report commissioned for the Commission on Private Schools in Ontario, 1984.

SPECIAL SCHOOLS

Education of the Deaf

Children with physical and mental challenges were cared for at home until the mid-nineteenth century, when special schools began to be established. The first school for the deaf in Ontario was the Upper Canada Institution for the Instruction of the Deaf and Dumb in Toronto, opened in 1858. This was later moved to Hamilton and renamed the Hamilton Institution for the Instruction of the Deaf and Dumb. In 1866 the school moved into Dundurn Castle, but it closed in 1870 when the

Ontario Institution for the Education and Instruction of the Deaf and Dumb was established in Belleville. This school continues to educate children today as the Sir James Whitney School for the Deaf.

Record Sources

RG 2-42-0-892 Estimates — maintenance and salaries. Ontario Institution for the Deaf and Dumb, 1905–1906. Available on microfilm.

RG 2-42-0-898 Admission lists, 1905, 1908 and 1909, Ontario Institution for the Deaf and Dumb. Available on microfilm.

RG 2-42-0-926 By-laws, list of teachers, general information about the Ontario Institution for the Deaf and Dumb, 1910. Available on microfilm.

There are additional files in RG 2-42 for the Ontario Institution for the Deaf and Dumb that deal with non-educational matters. But there are also a few files on individually named teachers. See the AO Descriptive Database.

Toronto School for the Instruction of the Deaf and Dumb, and Blind. *Semi-annual Report.* N.p.: 1864. CIHM microfiche series, no. A01044.

The Sir James Whitney School retains its own student records in Belleville.

The annual reports of the Ontario Institution for the Education and Instruction of the Deaf and Dumb were originally submitted

RAILWAY SCHOOLS

From 1926 to 1967, Canadian National and Canadian Pacific had school cars on their tracks that travelled a regular route with a teacher onboard to reach and teach the children of railroad workers, miners, loggers, hunters, trappers, and Aboriginal peoples. The Department of Education supplied teachers, books, and supplies; the railroad companies supplied the railway cars, maintained and serviced them, and moved them about the North. In the 1940s, there were seven schools cars on the rails, serving an area of more than 1,600 kilometres.

Children would walk, ski, snowshoe, canoe, and travel by dog sled over long distances to get a chance at the education offered by the railway schools. Most of the students did not have English as their first language and the travelling school was their first chance to have a formal education.

Two boys, David and Arthur Clement came 40 miles, set up an old tent in midwinter, thatched it with balsam boughs and lived there week by week as the School Car happened along at Ramsay.

— Inspector Gillies. "Memorandum for the Minister of Education Re. Railway School Cars. RG3-6-0-1032: Canadian National Railway School Car. RG3-6, Premier Howard Ferguson correspondence.

One of the original school cars still exists and has been restored for visitors in Clinton, Ontario (*www.schoolcar.ca*).

C.P.R. School Car No. 1, 1943. Teacher: W.H. McNally.

OISE Library, OHEC Collection. Photograph by Nunzio Goegan.

as part of the *Report of the Inspector of Prisons and Public Charities.* Later the *Report of the Superintendent of the Ontario School for the Deaf* became part of the *Annual Report of the Minister of Education.* "List of Pupils at the Ontario School for the Deaf." In *Annual Report of the Minister of Education*, beginning with 1918 and continuing through the 1920s.

Education of the Blind

Education for the blind came a little later, with the Ontario Institution for the Education and Instruction of the Blind opening in Brantford in 1872. It continues today as the W. Ross MacDonald School for the Blind.

Record Sources

RG 2-204 Ontario School for the Blind correspondence and administrative files, 1872–1978. These files cover the admission of pupils and the hiring of teachers, as well as student records and staff personnel files.

RG 2-377 Ontario School for the Blind Student Records, 1876–1945.

The Margaret Chandler Heritage House is maintained by the W. Ross MacDonald School as a museum of the early days of the school.

The annual reports of the Ontario Institution for the Education and Instruction of the Blind were originally submitted as part of the *Report of the Inspector of Prisons and Public Charities.* Later the *Report of the Superintendent of the Ontario School for the Blind* became part of the *Annual Report of the Minister of Education.*

"List of Pupils at the Ontario School for the Blind." In *Annual Report of the Minister of Education,* beginning with 1918 and continuing through the 1920s.

Dymond, A.H. *Ontario Institution for the Instruction and Education of the Blind: Where It Is, What It Is, What It Does.* Brantford, ON: Hurley & Watkins, 1902. CIHM microfiche series, no. 59231.

Further Reading

Chandler, M.R. *A Century of Challenge: The History of the Ontario School for the Blind.* Belleville, ON: Mika Publishing, 1980.

Carbin, Clifton F. *Deaf Heritage in Canada: A Distinctive, Diverse and Enduring Culture*. Toronto: McGraw-Hill Ryerson, 1996. This substantial account includes a detailed section on the education and schools for the deaf in Ontario.

——. *Samuel Thomas Greene: A Legend in the Nineteenth Century Deaf Community*. Belleville, ON: Epic Press, 2005. Contains both a biography of a prominent deaf educator and the history of the school for the deaf in Belleville.

Edquist, Verne. *Centre Walk: Former Students of the Ontario School for the Blind (the W. Ross Macdonald School) Recall School Memories*. North York, ON: Devondale, 1993.

Industrial Schools

The first industrial school in Ontario, the Victoria Industrial School for Boys, was opened in 1887 in Mimico, then a village near Toronto. It was closed in 1935. In 1892 the Alexandra Industrial School for Girls was established in Toronto. By 1894, nearly two hundred children, defined as neglected, abused, or delinquent, were housed in Ontario industrial schools. The Alexandra Industrial School amalgamated in 1936 with the Ontario Training School for Girls in Galt, later the Grandview Training School for Girls.

Related institutions, jails rather than schools, although some education was attempted, were the Industrial Refuge for Girls in Toronto, 1880–1905, and the Ontario Reformatory for Boys in Penetanguishene, 1859–1903.

Record Sources

RG 2-42-0-4813 Alexandria Industrial School, 1893. A list of students is included as part of the accounts provided to the provincial government. Available on microfilm

Victoria Industrial School.

RG 8-51 Victoria Industrial School Records, 1891–1935. Some lists of boys are included, along with additional information on some.

RG 8-52-2 Ontario Reformatory for Boys Inmates Histories, 1897–1903.

RG 20-166 Registers of the Ontario Industrial Refuge for Girls, 1880–1905. Available on microfilm.

McKinnon, Donald J. *The Victoria Industrial School and Its Late Superintendent: A Defence.* [Toronto?]: 1893. Addressed "to the members of the Toronto Public School Board, and of the Industrial School Association of Toronto."

CHAPTER 3

Schools

THE SCHOOL BUILDING

Of the public buildings in a community, the school building is the most important. If we are to cultivate the taste of the pupils and of the rest of the community, both it and its surroundings must be an example of taste, simplicity, and dignity in form and design.

— *Plans for Rural School Buildings with Estimates of Cost and Forms of Specifications and Agreements*. (Toronto: Ontario Department of Education, 1909), 5.

Although many of Ontario's early school buildings have disappeared, there are a sufficient number remaining, often now disguised as summer homes or restaurants, to give an idea of the physical surroundings experienced by pupils in the nineteenth and early twentieth century. Some have been preserved as school museums and visits are welcomed. See Appendix A for a list of some of the school museums operating in the province.

Printed by Order of the Legislative Assembly of Ontario, 1908.

The plan for a one-acre schoolyard from Improvement of School Grounds. Toronto.

ONE-ROOM SCHOOLS

In the nineteenth and for the early years of the twentieth century, one-room rural schools were a common sight in the Ontario landscape. The small grant provided by the 1816 Common School Act allowed for the building of these first small schoolhouses.

These schools were frequently extremely overcrowded, accommodating as many as sixty or more students with inadequate and uncomfortable furniture. Heat was provided by a wood- or coal-burning stove that the teacher had to maintain and water was obtained from a well, a pump, or some other external source. Outhouses were the only toilets. The teacher was often the janitor as well. Teaching aids were few and far between and often inexperienced teachers had the challenge of teaching pupils at many different grade and intellectual levels.

> In my one-room school I had twenty-two boys and no girls.... There was nothing up-to-date about our school. We had a long row of Coat hooks numbered with numerals cut out of calendars. We had a granite cup chained to a pump. There was no way to wash hands. The outhouses were outside.
>
> Quoted in Myrtle Fair, *I Remember the One-Room School* (Cheltenham, ON: Boston Mills Press, 1979), 18.

Getting to and from school could be a challenge for teachers and students in Ontario's winter. The teacher was expected to live in the community, at least during the school

A one-room school in Waterloo as depicted in the Education Department's annual report.

OISE Library, OHEC Collection.

week, so boarding with a local family — often a succession of them — was the norm. Loneliness was often the lot of the rural schoolteacher.

> In some school sections the label "suitcase teacher" was deadly and to be avoided at all costs. The suitcase teacher did her job well from Monday morning to Friday night. Then, hoping to have a little "life of her own," she went home for the weekend. "No!" said the school section. "The good teacher stays for the weekend and is part of the community for seven days!!
>
> — Quoted in Myrtle Fair, *I Remember the One-Room School* (Cheltenham, ON: Boston Mills Press, 1979), 34.

For all their drawbacks, many teachers and students retained fond memories of their years in the local one-room schools. With school consolidation and the move of the population from farms to the towns, these schools were left abandoned. Some were pulled down, or left to fall down, but a trip through the Ontario countryside gives evidence of the continued existence of many of these schoolhouses. The occasional one is now a school museum, but more often they have been reincarnated as private homes, cottages, or restaurants.

The architecture of the schoolhouse, the layout of the school grounds, and their effect on pupils were of considerable concern to early educators and administrators. There are a number of examples of beautifully illustrated treatises on the school architecture of Ontario that show both plans and elevation drawings for both new schools and also what were considered the best examples of existing buildings and grounds. It is worthwhile searching these for any local school of interest to you. They include:

Hodgins, J. George. *Hints and Suggestions on School Architecture and Hygiene with Plans and Illustrations.* Toronto: Education Department, 1886. Internet Archive.

Hodgins, J. George. *The School House: Its Architecture, External and Internal Arrangements, with Elevations and Plans for Public and High School Buildings, Together with Illustrated Papers on the Importance of School Hygiene and Ventilation, Also with Practical Suggestions as to School Grounds, School Furniture, Gymnastics, and the Uses and Value of School Apparatus.* Toronto: Copp, Clark, 1876. Internet Archive.

Improvement of School Grounds. Toronto: Printed by Order of the Legislative Assembly of Ontario, 1908. Internet Archive.

La Chance, W.W. *Modern Schoolhouses: With Plans and Illustrations of the Newest in Schoolhouse Architecture.* Ontario ed. Toronto: W. Briggs, 1919. Internet Archive.

Plans for Rural School Buildings with Estimates of Cost and Forms of Specifications and Agreements. Toronto: Ontario Department of Education, 1909. Internet Archive.

SCHOOL HISTORIES

There are many histories of individual schools and educational histories of a township or village that have been published over the years, often in conjunction with a school reunion or other commemorative event in a community. Frustratingly, many of these school histories, especially the earlier ones, do not list their sources. There are still more of these histories contained within the pages of general local histories, where a look back at education invariably occurs. Barbara Aitken's comprehensive bibliographies of Ontario local histories should be consulted to locate relevant publications:

Aitken, Barbara B. *Local Histories of Ontario Municipalities Published in the Years 1957–1972.* Revised and enlarged edition. Kingston, ON: Kingston Public Library Board, 1972.

——. *Local Histories of Ontario Municipalities, 1951–1977: A Bibliography, with Representative Trans-Canada Locations of Copies.* Toronto: Ontario Library Association, 1978.

——. *Local Histories of Ontario Municipalities, 1977–1987: A Bibliography, with Representative Cross-Canada Locations of Copies.* Toronto: Ontario Library Association, 1989.

——. *Local Histories of Ontario Municipalities, 1987–1997: A Bibliography, with Representative Cross-Canada Locations of Copies.* Toronto: Ontario Genealogical Society, 1999.

From the author's collection.

Central School, Oil Springs, Ontario.

——. *Local Histories of Ontario Municipalities, 1997–2007: A Bibliography.* Toronto: Ontario Genealogical Society, 2009.

You should also consult the two-volume work, *A Bibliography of Ontario History 1867–1976: Cultural, Economic, Political, Social,* by Olga Bishop (Toronto, ON: University of Toronto Press, 1980), especially the section on education in volume one and the section on local history in volume two.

The list of school histories that follows is by no means complete and it appears that to this point there is no compilation of all the school histories that exist. Many are published and sold locally and never find their way to larger libraries (nor indeed to Library and Archives Canada, in some cases). So, once again, a visit to the public library or archives in any area is likely to unearth further accounts of local schools. In fact, visiting or contacting the local library or archives first for all local school records is a good strategy. They will often house the education records themselves and, if not, will almost certainly know where

74

the records (if they exist) currently are. At a minimum, these local institutions will have a file on local education.

When looking for the school an ancestor attended, it is useful to keep the history of school administration in mind, particularly when it comes to rural schools. The Common School Act of 1850 created School Sections (S.S.), small units of administration, typically three to five miles square. In the early years of the twentieth century, these small rural schools began to be regarded as expensive to run and maintain, and the education they were able to provide was seen as inferior to that of the schools in urban centres. After the Consolidated Schools Act of 1919, the process of closing and consolidating schools began; a process that was as unpopular then as it is now, to the extent that the Department of Education had to issue explanatory pamphlets:

> There is in the process of evolution in this Province a new educational institution, which will provide for farm boys and girls, primary and secondary education in a consolidated school owned and conducted by the community, in which the instruction and course of study are closely adjusted to the lives that the pupils are later to lead.

> — Ontario Department of Education.
> *The Consolidation of Rural Schools.*
> (Toronto: Kings' Printer, 1922), 23.

The government gave substantial grants to school boards to pay for consolidation and to help with the cost of transporting pupils to the new schools. Two or more townships might also have decided to join school sections, forming Union School Sections.

In the 1940s, Township School Areas were created to promote further consolidation. These were units of school administration "comprising two or more contiguous rural school sections in the same township or adjacent townships, or comprising such rural sections along with one or more adjacent villages or towns."

Before the advent of Township School Areas, there were 5,747 School Sections; in 1948 there were just 499 Township School Areas. Further consolidation occurred in the 1960s and continues today. All the names of the Township School Areas can be found in *The Township School Area in Ontario*, Ontario Department of Education, Toronto: King's Printer, 1948 (definition quoted from page 3).

This administrative history means that if school records do not appear in the archives or library that you expect, try looking further afield, beyond present-day boundaries.

Another fact to keep in mind when searching for school histories is that many schools were known by those who attended them, not by their official name, but by a local designation. Cairnbrogie School, the subject of one of the histories listed on page 83, is one; officially its designation was S.S. #1, Wainwright Township, but it was known as Cairnbrogie School and this was the title given to its published history.

Along with school histories and local histories, you should seek out the diaries and memoirs of pioneers and the old-timers of a district. These often include a lively account of the author's school days along with the location of schools and the names of teachers and fellow pupils. For example:

> I went no more to school until "our boys" had returned from the war, which school opened the summer I was six years old. It was taught by the Mr. Barber ... who had lost some of his fingers from one hand, which constituted a justification of his natural indisposition to work.... Barber

wanted employment; he had some little education, and a school was needed in our section of the town for those who did not attend the District Grammar School, which was mostly appropriated by the descendants of the Family Compact.

— Carroll, John, *My Boy Life: Presented in a Succession of True Stories* (Toronto: William Briggs, 1882), 265. Internet Archive.

See also Gourley, Robert. *Statistical Account of Upper Canada* (London: Simpkin & Marshall, 1822. Abridged edition. Toronto: McClelland and Stewart, 1974). In 1817, Robert Gourley, a visitor to Canada, sent out thirty-one queries to the most prominent men in each municipality; one of these queries related to education and schools. The answers to this query are summarized by Hodgins in his *Documentary History of Upper Canada*, vol. 1: 123–28. The *Documentary History* should also be searched for the variety of other accounts of early schools included. For example: "Schools in Existence in Upper Canada During the Early Part of 1800," vol. 1: 30–35; "Early School Days in Aldborough, Talbot Settlement, 1816–1820," vol. 1: 162–67; "Early Establishment of Schools in Upper Canada, 1813–1831," vol. 1: 319–21 and "Early Schools in the Village of Smith Falls, 1832" in vol. 2: 125.

See also **RG 2 87** — Department of Education Local School Histories and Teaching Experiences Files, 1846–1896, which documents the teaching experiences of some nineteenth-century Ontario teachers and the early history of schools in some towns and townships in the province. It is available on microfilm and an online finding aid is available. As part of the work of compiling his monumental *Documentary History of Education in Upper Canada*, John George Hodgins requested teachers throughout

Ontario to send him accounts of their personal experience and the histories of their local schools. Their responses are to be found in these files.

There are additional accounts of teaching and school histories in **Fonds F 1207**, the John G. Hodgins fonds.

"Extracts from the Reports of Local Superintendents of Common Schools and Boards of School Trustees in Upper Canada, Relative to the State and Progress of Elementary Education in Their Respective Townships, Cities, Towns and Villages...." In *Annual Reports of the Minister of Education*. (Title varies; 1851 to about 1900. Not included in every annual report.)

> I cannot speak very flatteringly of the schools in this township during the past year; there are, however, several which are seldom surpassed.... There is a want of interest on the part of many parents in the intellectual culture of their children to which the non-attendance of children must in general be attributed.
>
> — *Annual Report of the Minister of Education*, 1861: 168.

General School Histories

Eames, Frank. "Pioneer Schools of Upper Canada." Ontario Historical Society *Papers and Records* 18 (1920), 91–103. Indicates when and where in Upper Canada the first schools were organized from 1786–1833.

MacDougall, J.B. *Building the North*. Toronto: McClelland & Stewart, 1919. A detailed history of education and individual schools in northern Ontario. The author was a master at

North Bay Normal School and inspector of public schools for New Ontario from 1904 to 1911.

Milburn, G. "Ontario Grammar Schools, 1853–1871." Master's thesis, University of Durham, 1960.

Algoma District

Dixon, Catharine. *As It Happened: The Founding of Elliot Lake Secondary School.* Elliot Lake, ON: Gillidix Publishing, 2001.

Strum, Merritt. *A Backward Glance Through School History (Central Algoma).* Bruce Mines, ON: The Author, 2005.

Brant County

Files, Angela. *The Rural Public Schools of Brant County.* Brantford, ON: Brant County Branch, Ontario Genealogical Society, 1985.

Webster, J.C. *Rural Schools of South Dumfries Township: A History of Rural Schools in South Dumfries Township, Ontario to 1961.* Brantford, ON: Brant Historical Society, 1992.

Bruce County

Culbert, Mary and Murray Culbert. *Memories are Made of This: A Tribute to the Teachers of Ripley and Huron Township.* Ripley, ON: The Authors, 1994.

History of Schools of Bruce Township. Bruce Township, ON: Bruce Township School Area Board, 1965.

History of the School Sections of Tiverton and Kincardine Township from Their Founding Until the Formation of the Kincardine Township — Tiverton Public School Area. N.p.: 1967.

History of the Schools in the Culross-Teeswater School Area. Teeswater, ON: Culross-Teeswater School Area Board, 1967.

McLaughlin, Olive. *The History of Scone School Section.* Walkerton, ON: Herald-Times Press, 1975.

Carleton County

Cummings, H.R., and W.T Macskimming. *The City of Ottawa Public Schools: A Brief History.* Ottawa, ON: Ottawa Board of Education, 1971.

Executive Committee of the O.C. Ex-Pupils' Association, comp. *A History of the Ottawa Collegiate Institute 1843–1903.* Ottawa: Mortimer Co., 1904. Internet Archive.

Hessel, Peter. *The Evolution of a School: A History of the Crichton Street Public School in the Ottawa Suburb of New-Edinburgh.* Ottawa, ON: Crichton Home & School Association, 1964.

Keith, Janet. *The Collegiate Institute Board of Ottawa: A Short History, 1843–1969.* Ottawa, ON: Ottawa Collegiate Institute Board, 1969.

Lisgar Collegiate Institute. *Lisgar Collegiate Centenary, 1843–1943.* Ottawa, ON: Lisgar Collegiate Centenary, Editorial and Publications Committee, 1943.

Mark, C.E. *The Public Schools of Ottawa: A Survey.* Ottawa, ON: Pattison Printers, 1918. Internet Archive.

Uren, Janet B. *Voices from Elmwood School, 1915–2000.* Ottawa, ON: Elmwood School, 2000.

Dundas County

Harkness, A. *Iroquois High School, 1845–1895: A Story of Fifty Years.* Toronto: W. Briggs, 1896. CIHM microfiche series, no. 05363.

Durham County

History of Mitchell's Corners Public Schools, 1861–1978. N.p.: Mitchell's Corner's Home and School Association, 1978.

Elgin County

Fife, Margaret G., and Elyse McKillop. *Historical Sketches of Southwold Township School Sections.* N.p.: 1971.

Essex County

Mills, Harold. *History of Negro Settlement Schools of Colchester Township.* N.p.: 1959.

Sixty Years of Secondary Education in Essex County, 1919 to 1979: A Diamond Jubilee Project of the Secondary School Teachers' Federation. Windsor, ON: Preney Print Litho, 1980.

A Story of Public Schools in Colchester South Township. Harrow, ON: Harrow and Colchester South Township School Area Board, 1966.

Frontenac County

"The Bell and Laing School Papers." Lennox and Addington Historical Society, *Papers and Records* 5 (1914) 6–27. Internet Archive.

Hogeboom. Alice E. *Chalk Dust: The History of Education in Kingston Township.* Kingston, ON, 1968.

Lapp, D.A. "The Schools of Kingston: Their First Hundred and Fifty Years." Master's thesis, Queen's University, 1937.

Smith, F.P. "Early Schools in Kingston." *Historic Kingston* 5 (October 1956), 25.

Sydenham High School, 1873–1967. Sydenham, ON: Sydenham High School History Book Committee, 1967.

Grey County

A History of Dufferin School, 1889–1973. Owen Sound, ON: S. Brown Printers, 1973.

Hubbert, Mildred Young. *The Little Schools of Grey.* N.p.: 1982.

McEachern, J. Garry. *Upwards to the Stars: A Social History of Secondary Education in Meaford.* Meaford, ON: The Author, 1991.

Sturgeon, Donald R. *Just Yesterday: A Twenty-Five Year History of Education in Grey County, 1950 to 1975.* Markdale, ON: Grey County Board of Education, 1985.

Haldimand County

High, Norman Hervey. "A Study of Educational Opportunity in the Provincially-Controlled Schools of Haldimand County, Ontario." Ph.D. dissertation, Cornell University, 1950.

MacDonald, Cheryl, Mary Sheppard, and Dana Stavinga. *Rural Schools of Haldimand.* Selkirk, ON: North Erie Shore Historical Society, 1997.

Ufland, Vina R. *History of the Schools of St. Vincent Township and Other Chronicles, 1847–1967.* Meaford, ON: Township of St. Vincent, 1970.

Hastings County

Boyce, Gerald E. "The Bayside Property and School, 1784–1874." *Ontario History* 64, no. 4 (December, 1972), 181–200.

Huron County

Grant, Angus Murray. *From Log School to United Church: From Brewster to Grand Bend*. N.p.: 1964.
Green, Gavin Hamilton. *The Old Log School*. Toronto: Natural History/Natural Heritage Inc., 1992.

Kenora District

Morton, Russell. *Cairnbrogie School: Tales of a Northern Township*. Richmond Hill, ON: Northpine Publishing, 1999.

Lambton County

The Old Landmarks: A Brief Historical Sketch of the Schools in Bosanquet, Arkona, Thedford, Grand Bend, Kettle Point, Forest. Forest, ON: Forest Free Press, 1971.
Sarnia, Ontario, Bright's Grove School. Centennial Committee. *Centennial, 1863–1963*. Sarnia, ON, 1963.

Lanark County

Smith, Claudia. *Country School Days, 1830s–1960s*. Almonte, ON: C.J. Smith, 2007.
Sutherland, Lloyd C. *Yearning for Learning: The Story of Education in Lanark County, 1804–1867*. Toronto, 1980.
Sutherland, Lloyd C. *Yearning for Learning: The Story of Education in Lanark County, 1804–1967*. Toronto: n.d.
Williams, M.E. "Early History of Education in the District of Bathurst." Master's thesis, University of Ottawa, 1951.

Leeds and Grenville County

Eames, Frank. "Gananoque's First Public School, 1816." Ontario Historical Society *Papers and Records* 17 (1919), 90–105.

Hughes, Alice M. *Dear Old Golden Rule Days: A History of the One-Room Schools of Wolford Township.* N.p.: A.M. Hughes and N.H. Dulmage, 2004.

Sweet's Corners Elementary School Reunion Committee. *Schools in the Township of Rear of Leeds and Lansdowne.* Kingston, ON: Brown & Martin, 1973.

Warner, Howard W. *A History of Read's Public School, S.S. No. 2 & 30, South Augusta, Ontario.* Ottawa, ON, 1979.

Lennox and Addington County

Morton, Ross C. *Story of the Conway Public School, 1875–1966 and Memories of My Boyhood during the 1930s.* Bath, ON: South Fredericksburgh Heritage Committee, 1997.

Lincoln County

Carnochan, Janet. "The Early Schools of Niagara." Niagara Historical Society *Report and Papers* 6 (1900), 37–38, 43–44. CIHM microfiche series, no. 03843.

Grant, Gordon. *A History of Caistor Schools, Caistor Township.* N.p.: Caistor Central School, 1967.

History of the Elementary Schools of the Inspectorate of Lincoln No. 2 and Welland No. 6 at the Time of the Centenary of Lincoln and Welland Counties, 1956. St. Catharines, ON, 1956.

Love, James, ed. *Education in the Niagara Peninsula: Tenth Annual Niagara Peninsula History Conference, Brock University, April 30– May 1, 1988.* St. Catharines, ON: Vanwell Publishing, 1991.

Victoria School Diamond Jubilee Committee. *Victoria School Diamond Jubilee, 1912–1972.* St. Catharines, ON: Advance Printing, 1972.

Middlesex County

McCutcheon, F.W.C. "The London Grammar School and the Collegiate Institute." *Transactions of the London and Middlesex Historical Society,* part 10 (1919), 31.

Muskoka District

Denniss, Gary. *A Brief History of Schools in Muskoka.* Bracebridge, ON: Herald-Gazette Press, 1972. Our Roots.
——. *Educating Muskoka District.*Self-published, 1999. Our Roots.
——. *The Educational Heritage of Muskoka.* Self-published, 2001.

Norfolk County

Bannister, John. *Early Educational History of Norfolk County.* Toronto: University of Toronto Press, 1926.

Ontario County

Ross, J. Douglas. *Education in Oshawa: From Settlement to City.* Oshawa, ON: Ontario County Board of Education, 1970.

Oxford County

Embro Centennial and Zorra Old Boys and Girls Reunion, 1858–1958. Tillsonburg, ON: McCready's Printing Co., 1958.
Walker's School: S.S. No. 1, West Zorra, 1869–1966. Woodstock,

ON: Nethercott Printing, 1966.

S.S. No. 3, West Zorra — Bennington School, 1864–1966. N.p.: 1966.

S.S. No. 4, West Zorra — Harrington West: Old Boys and Girls Reunion 1966. N.p.: 1966.

S.S. No. 5, West Zorra — Codys' Corner, 1848–1966. N.p.: 1966.

History of S.S. No. 6, West Zorra —Youngsville 1866–1966. N.p.: 1966.

S.S. No. 8, West Zorra — Golspie School, 1867–1966. N.p.: Historical Committee, 1966.

A Century at Elmsdale School: S.S. No. 10, West Zorra, 1866–1966. Woodstock, ON: Nethercott Printing, 1966.

Parry Sound District

Lee, Patricia. *The Lunch Bucket Chronicles: A History of Rural Public Schools in East Parry Sound.* Carp, ON: Gai-Garet Design and Publications, 1990.

Superannuated Teachers of Ontario. Parry Sound Branch. *Then and Now: West Parry Sound Schools, 1865–1981.* N.p.: 1982.

Peel County

Delaney, Ruth, and Lois Russell. *Down Memory Lane: S.S. No. 11: Chinguacousy School Reunion 1866–1961.* N.p.: Chinguacousy Reunion Committee, 1992.

Grahamsville S.S. 24 1821–1960. N.p.: Historical Book Committee, 1960.

Hesp, Murray. *Bolton School Days.* Bolton, ON: Leavens Printers and Publishers, 1970.

——. *The School on the Hill: Known as Caledon East School.* Caledon East, ON: Caledon East School Reunion Committee, 2006.

Patterson, Howard S. "A Brief History of the Dingle School (School Section Number 11, Township of Albion)." An Essay

Submitted.... [for the] Degree of Bachelor of Education, Brock University, 1961. Typescript. Region of Peel Archives.

Speers, J. Alvin. *Reminiscence re S.S. #8 Caledon, Ontario, on Occasion of Reunion 2001: "Looking Back 64 Years."* Calgary, AB: Aardvark Enterprises, 2001.

Perth County

Ahrens, Martin and others. *Stratford Central Secondary School, 1853–1968: A History.* Stratford, ON: B-H Press, 1968.

Malvern, K.D., ed. *Stratford Central Secondary School: Its History, 1853–1979.* Stratford, ON, 1979.

Mornington Centennial and Milverton Old Boys & Girls Reunion, 1857–1957: A Centenary of Progress, August 2 to August 5. Souvenir booklet and program. N.p.: 1959.

Stanley, J.R. *Our St. Mary's Schools: An Historical Sketch.* St. Mary's, ON: The *St. Mary's Journal, circa* 1909. CIHM microfiche series, no. 87521.

Peterborough County

Bolton, R.J. *History of Central Public School, Peterborough, 1860–1960.* Unpublished manuscript. Trent University Archives, Peterborough.

Londerville, J.J.D. "Schools of Peterborough: Their First Hundred Years." Master's thesis, Queen's University, 1942.

Prince Edward County

As the Twig is Bent — So Grows the Tree: A Story of Prince Edward County Schools. Bloomfield, ON: Quinte Educational Museum and Archives, 1984.

Rainey, Daniel. *The Victoria Schoolhouse: A Sense of Community.* Ameliasburg, ON: Quinte Educational Museum and Archives, 2006.

Wilkinson, Cecil E. *History of Education in Ontario: A Historical Sketch of S.S. II Sophiasburg Township, Prince Edward County.* Woodville, ON, 1965.

Willcox, C. *Centennial Booklet, Picton (Ont.). Collegiate and Vocational Institute, 1834–1934.* N.p.: 1934.

Renfrew County

Ross, A.H.D. *A Short History of the Arnprior High School, 1865–1922.* N.p.: 1922.

Simcoe County

Blackburn, Helen Emmett. *Has the Bell Rung Yet?: A History of Education in Creemore and Surrounding Area.* Creemore, ON: Curiosity House, 1979. Our Roots.

Campbell, Howard, Mrs. Victor Ross, and Mrs. Albert Pearsall. *A History of Oro Schools, 1836–1966.* N.p.: Oro Township School Board, 1966.

Wilcox, Leslie F. *School Section No. 11, Tecumseth Township: A History of Its 120 Years, 1837–1957.* Bradford, ON: Bradford Witness Pub., 1958.

Stormont County

Spragge, George W. "The Cornwall Grammar School under John Strachan, 1803–1812." *Ontario Historical Society Papers and Records* 34 (1942), 63–84.

Thunder Bay District

Turk, Linda and Art Gunnell. *Five Miles and All Uphill: Early Schools in the Lakehead and Area.* Kakabeka Falls, ON: Mile Hill Press, 2001.

Victoria County

Nicholson, Alexander Massey, and Larry Skitch, eds. *Sentimental Journey: Secondary School Life in North Victoria County.* Fenelon Falls, ON: Reunion Committee, Fenelon Falls Secondary School, 1993.

Robinson, Ralph. *Educating Victoria County: A Local History of Education.* Lindsay, ON: Tri-M Pub, 1987.

Waterloo County

Bloomfield, Elizabeth, and Linda Foster. *Waterloo Township Schools, 1842–1972.* Guelph, ON: Caribou Imprints, 1995.

Bowman, Henry B. "Miss Alma Crawforth and the Continuation School in Elmira." *Waterloo Historical Society* 61 (1973), 24–28.

Galt Collegiate Institute Semi-Centennial and Tassie Old Boy's Re-Union. Galt, 1902.

Johnston, May A. *The Trail of the Slate: A History of Early Education in Waterloo County, 1802–1912.* Waterloo, ON: The Author, 1975.

Klinck, George. *The Development and Progress of Education in Elmira and the Vicinity.* Elmira, ON: The Author, 1938.

EDUCATION AND ONTARIO FAMILY HISTORY

Welland County

History of the Elementary Schools of the Inspectorate of Lincoln No. 2 and Welland No. 6 at the Time of the Centenary of Lincoln and Welland Counties, 1956. St. Catharines, ON, 1956.

Lees, John M. *Thorold Secondary School, 1857–1975: An Illustrated History.* Pelham, ON: Canada Year Book Service, 1975.

Wellington County

Beattie, David M. *A History of S.S. No. 4, Nichol Township, County of Wellington.* N.p.: 1959.

Broughton, Ethel, comp. *A Historical Sketch of S.S. No. 5, Erin, County of Wellington: Coningsby Public School, Coningsby, Ontario.* N.p.: 1962.

Hale, Lynda, Joy Nicol, and Carol Patterson. *The Little Red School House.* N.p.: 1973.

Mack, Hazel L. *S.S. No. 1, Eramosa Township: One Hundred and Twenty Years of School History.* N.p.: 1962.

Maddock, F.L. *Pioneer Days in School Section No. 12, Puslinch Town.* Guelph, ON, 1939.

Shutt, Greta Mary. *The High Schools of Guelph: Being the Story of the Wellington District Grammar School, Guelph Grammar School, Guelph High School, and Guelph's Collegiate Institutes.* Guelph, ON: Board of Education for the City of Guelph, 1961.

Tanguay, Suzanne I. *The History and Development of Welland High and Vocational School, 1854–1979.* Welland, ON, 1979.

Wentworth County

Aikman, Murray W., and Robert J. Williamson. *The Board of Education for the City of Hamilton, 1847–1997.* Hamilton,

ON: The Board of Education for the City of Hamilton Archives, 1997.

Aikman, Murray W., ed. *Strathcona Remembers.* [Hamilton, ON?]: Strathcona Reunion Committee, 1984.

Davey, Ian E. "School Reform and School Attendance: The Hamilton Central School, 1853–1851." In *Education and Social Change: Themes from Ontario's Past,* edited by Michael B. Katz and Paul H. Mattingly, New York: New York University Press, 1975: 294–314.

Smith, J.H. *The Central School Jubilee Re-Union (Hamilton, Ont.), 1853–1903.* Hamilton, ON: Spectator Printing, 1905.

Spalding, L.T. *History and Romance of Education (Hamilton), 1816–1950.* Hamilton, ON, 1950.

York County

Berry, Susan. *A History of Education in the Lakeshore Area: (Mimico/New Toronto/Long Branch).* Toronto: Wylie Press, 1967.

Etobicoke Board of Education. *Reminiscing: Memories About Education in Etobicoke and the Lakeshore Areas.* N.p.: 1981.

Farrow, Clare. *The Origin and Demise of New Toronto Secondary School.* N.p.: 1983.

Hathaway, Ernest J. "Early Schools of Toronto." Ontario Historical Society *Papers and Records* 23 (1926), 312–27.

History of Toronto and County of York, Ontario: Containing an Outline ... With the Townships, Towns, Villages, Churches, Schools.... Toronto: C. Blackett Robinson, 1885. Two volumes. Internet Archive.

Jacques, Marjorie. *A History of Holland Landing Public School.* Richmond Hill, ON: York County Board of Education, 1975.

Medland, Harvey. *Minerva's Diary: A History of Jarvis Collegiate Institute.* Belleville, ON: Mika Pub. Co., 1979.

North York Board of Education. *150 Years of Progress: Education in North York*. North York, ON, 1968.

Oral History Project, Toronto District School Board. *School Days: Recollections of Toronto Schools*. Toronto: Learnxs Foundation in co-operation with the Toronto District School Board, 2003.

Park School. Biographies of individual schools under the Toronto Board of Education, no. 2. Toronto: Bureau of Municipal Research, 1921. Internet Archive.

Report of the Past History and Present Condition of the Common or Public Schools of the City of Toronto. Toronto: Lovell & Gibson, 1859. CIHM microfiche series, no. 34150.

Spragge, G.W. "The Upper Canada Central School." Ontario Historical Society *Papers and Records* 22 (1937), 171–91.

The Sunnylea Story, 1908–1985. Toronto, 1985.

Toronto Board of Education. *Report of the Past History and Present Condition of the Common or Public Schools of Toronto*. Toronto: Lovell & Gibson, 1859.

Vance, Bruce. *Reverend George Okill Stuart and the Home District Public School in the Town of York, 1807–1811*. Education in Toronto Board of Education Public School No. 4. Toronto: Sesquicentennial Museum and Archives, Toronto Board of Education, 1995.

———. *Reverend Doctor John Strachan, Reverend Samuel Armour and the Old Blue School, 1812–1825*. Education in Toronto Board of Education Public School No. 5. Toronto: Sesquicentennial Museum and Archives, Toronto Board of Education, 1995.

———. *Reverend Doctor Thomas Phillips and the Royal Grammar School at York, 1825–1829*. Education in Toronto Board of Education Public School No. 6. Toronto: Sesquicentennial Museum and Archives, Toronto: Board of Education, 1996.

Wattie, Dora E. *One Hundred Years, a Retrospect, 1857–1957: Weston Grammar School to Weston Collegiate and Vocational School.* Toronto: Chromo Lithographing Co., 1957.

Weaver, Laura. *German Mills School, 1874–1974: Centennial.* Thornhill, ON, 1974.

York Street School. Biographies of individual schools under the Toronto Board of Education No. 1. Toronto: Bureau of Municipal Research, 1920.

CHAPTER 4

Teachers and Teaching

I came out from Ireland in 1851, and taught for five months in Clark Township in a Log School House. The Reverend William Ormiston, who was the School Superintendent gave me the Government Grant. There were no Maps in the School and I taught from any Books that were brought to the School by the Pupils.

In 1852, I taught in a Log School House in Number Seven, Cavan, where there were no conveniences for teaching. The Books used were the Irish National Series, Morrison's Geography.

In 1851 [*sic*] I became the Teacher of School Section Number Seven, Nepean, the largest and wealthiest Section in the Township. The School House was well-furnished with Desks, Seats, Maps, and Blackboards, but the School Building was too small for the number of Pupils attending — one hundred and twenty on the roll, with an average attendance of eighty...

I taught this School for seven years, and turned out three Second Class Teachers from among the Pupils. My salary was two hundred and forty dollars per annum.

— Fallow Field, 1896.
" Patrick O'Meara. Reminiscences of
Superannuated Teachers, 1852." Quoted in
J. George Hodgins, *Documentary History of
Education in Upper Canada*, vol. 28 (Toronto:
King's Printer, 1876), 245.

THE TRAINING OF TEACHERS

The first teachers in the Common Schools of Ontario were hired simply because they were on the spot and could demonstrate at least a rudimentary knowledge of reading, writing, and arithmetic. They were appointed and dismissed by the elected school trustees, were poorly paid, and usually abandoned teaching after a short period. In 1838, Anna Jameson, travelling around Upper Canada, saw and commented on the state of teaching:

Who that could earn a subsistence in any other way would be a schoolmaster in the wilds of Upper Canada? Ill-fed, ill-clothed, ill-paid, or not paid at all — boarded at the homes of different farmers in turn — I found indeed some few men, poor creatures! Always either Scotch or Americans — and totally unfit for the office they had undertaken.

— Anna Jameson, *Winter Studies and Summer Rambles in Canada*, vol. 2 (London: Saunders and Otley, 1838), 23.

The first Common School Act of 1816 had decreed that teachers had to be British subjects or have taken the oath of allegiance. In 1843, a revision of the Common School Act included, for the first time, a provision for the formal training of teachers. A "model school" was to be established in each township, later each county, the teacher of which was to give instruction to other teachers in the township. However, these model schools "succeeded only in handing over the vast majority of schools to the half-trained and the immature," and so did not prove to be a success. Although the system was expanded in 1871, it was discontinued in 1907.

TEACHER SALARIES

Throughout the nineteenth century and for much of the twentieth, the amount they received in pay was a significant issue for Ontario teachers. In the early years of the province, salaries were not only low, but there was the problem of collecting them in a system that required parents to contribute part of the remuneration a teacher received. Christopher Julian arrived in Canada in 1834 and taught for six months in a school six miles outside of Cobourg "at 10 dollars per month with board and lodging."

I presented my school report to the Board of Education at the quarter sessions, where

I received 18 dollars as a gratuity from the Government for my six months' teaching. The 29th, I went to collect the remainder of my school money — in general it was pretty well paid. I got it all except from three persons — one of them owed me three dollars, and refused to pay altogether. He said I should take law proceedings for the recovery of it, as he had no means of paying me. This is what is called a "Yankee trick," for he was aware that I would not then lose time to sue him. Another owed me five dollars, but he said he could not pay until the harvest, and proposed to give me his note, payable in three months, which I accepted; and left it with Mr. William Kelly of Haldamond [*sic*] to receive the amt. for me, together with two dollars more for another.

— Christopher Julian's diary, 14 July
1835, Private Collection, Toronto.

Other occupations were better paid than teachers, even labourers and domestic servants, lamented one school inspector in his report in 1882. The many females who joined the ranks of teachers — it was one of the few acceptable professions for women — had the effect of driving salaries down as they were paid much less than their male counterparts. Observers had no problem with the inequity between the salaries for male and female teachers as women were considered to be temporary members of the workforce and as such, worth less.

Average Salary in 1900

Beginning female teacher in Toronto	$324
Charwoman at Post Office	$321
Street Sweeper	$421
Labourer at Stock Yards	$546

Doris French Shackleton, *High Button Bootstraps: Federation of Women Teachers' Associations of Ontario, 1918-1968* (Toronto: Ryerson Press, 1968): 20.

Salaries of Teachers in Toronto

Date	Women	Men
1858	$240–$400	$520–$700
1870	$220–$400	$600–$700
1881	$200–$600	$750–1,100
1901	$225–$675	$600–$900
1910	$400–$900	$900–$1,400
1920	$1,000–$2,000	$1,625–$2,500
1930	$1,000–$2,400	$1,200–$3,000

Elizabeth Graham, "Schoolmarms and Early Teaching in Ontario," in *Women at Work: Ontario, 1850–1930* (Toronto: Canadian Women's Educational Press, 1974), 194.

Rural salaries were significantly lower than those offered in schools in large city centres, like Toronto.

Average Rural Teacher's Salary in Ontario

Date	Women	Men
1870		
country schools	$187	$260
town schools	$200	$450
1901	$262	$359
1928	$609	$743

Elizabeth Graham,"Schoolmarms and EarlyTeaching in Ontario," in *Women at Work: Ontario, 1850 – 1930* (Toronto: Canadian Women's Educational Press, 1974): 194.

Organization by the women teachers and then by teachers as a unified group eventually led to wage parity between males and females and to a salary level that recognized their education and professionalism.

The revised Common School Act of 1846 provided funds for the support of a "normal school" for elementary teacher training, to be founded in Toronto. The word *normal* in this context meant "according to rule or principle."

In 1847, the Provincial Normal School, as it was first known, opened in the old Government House, moving in 1852 to a new, purpose-built normal school with associated boys' and girls' model schools at the corner of Church and Gould streets in Toronto. A certificate to recognize the graduates of the normal school was introduced in 1853. A First Class Certificate was awarded after two sessions at normal school; the Second Class Certificate after at least one session. A session covered much the same time period as the current academic year, September to July. The following is an excerpt from the *Annual Report* of the Minister of Education for 1848:

> That all Candidates for admission into the [Normal] School must comply with the following conditions: — [1] They must be, at least sixteen years of age; [2] — must produce a certificate of good moral character, signed by the Clergyman or minister of the religious persuasion with which they are connected; [3] — must be able to read and write intelligibly, and be acquainted with the simple rules of arithmetic; [4] — must sign a declaration of their intention to devote themselves to the profession of School-teaching....

But during this period, the majority of teachers in the schools still had no formal training and possessed only the certificate that the board of public instruction in each county was authorized to issue after examining a teaching candidate.

In 1871, the standards for certificates were raised. A county board of examiners was created that could award two classes of certificates — "lower" and "higher" — with the Higher Certificate being equivalent to a Second Class Certificate earned at a normal school. The Lower Class Certificate was valid for only three years. Some districts, particularly in the northern parts of the province, were unable to support a normal school. To provide teachers in these areas with at least a modest level of basic, practical training, a model school scheme was again attempted.

In 1896, district model schools were established in the districts of Thunder Bay, Algoma, Parry Sound, and Nipissing;

these were merged in 1908 into a broader system of provincial model schools, of which there were fifteen by 1912. Here teachers could obtain a Third Class Certificate valid for five years. Although it was the assumption that holders of a Third Class Certificate would continue on to Normal School, most left teaching after the expiry of their certificates. Low pay and inadequate working conditions made teaching less attractive than other professions.

In 1956, the First Class Certificate was replaced by the Elementary School Teacher's Certificate. The transfer of teachers' colleges into the university system and the requirement of a university degree as well as teacher training qualifications for elementary school teachers began in 1969. By 1973 a university degree was required for all students seeking to teach at the elementary level.

Gladstone Avenue School, Toronto, 1902.

The Training of Secondary-School Teachers

For the most part, until the 1880s, a university degree was thought sufficient for anyone teaching at a grammar school in Ontario. After an unsuccessful experiment with training institutes in selected collegiate institutes, a School of Pedagogy was formed in association with the Toronto Normal School, offering advanced-level courses suitable for high-school teachers. In 1897, the school was moved to Hamilton and renamed the Ontario Normal College. The college closed in 1906, and the training was taken over by the faculties of education at the University of Toronto and Queen's University in Kingston. These, too, were closed in 1920, although the University of Toronto retained a renamed Ontario College of Education (OCE), which was funded separately by the province. All students at the college were required to have a university arts degree before being admitted.

The Ontario College of Education was the only institution authorized to provide high-school teacher training in the province, although students could take an option that allowed them to teach at the elementary level. This monopoly ended in 1965 when Althouse College of Education, affiliated with the University of Western Ontario in London, and McArthur College of Education, affiliated with Queen's University, were established. In 1966, the OCE once again came under the complete jurisdiction of the University of Toronto, and in 1972 was renamed the Faculty of Education.

Toronto Normal School.

The cast of "She Stoops to Conquer," Faculty of Education, University of Toronto, 1916.

RECORDS FOR TEACHER TRAINING

Normal School/Teachers College Yearbooks and Histories

The records for the normal schools after 1953, known as teachers' colleges, range from records of applications, attendance, and examination results to student yearbooks and written histories. Yearbooks can be especially interesting, typically containing the photographs of all classes, sports teams, and hobby societies, along with essays, poetry, humorous skits, and reviews of the school year written by the students. Many of the teacher training institutions were established well into the time-frame that is covered by privacy restrictions, so yearbooks may be the only sources open to searching. Following is a list of the source material available for each institution.

Hamilton Normal School, 1908–1979
From 1974–1979 known as the Hamilton Campus of the Ontario Teacher Education College.

Yearbook
OHEC 1920/21–1972/1973 irregular holdings

AO RG 2-340 Hamilton Normal School Student Records, 1908–1977

> **AO RG 2-340-1** Hamilton Normal School Admissions Register

> **AO RG 2-340-2** Hamilton Normal School Entrance Registers

A photograph of one of the many societies in the yearbook of the Hamilton Normal School, 1920/21.

AO RG 2-340-3 Hamilton Normal School Student Signature and Address Register

AO RG 2-340-4 Hamilton Normal School Oaths of Allegiance and Office Register

AO RG 2-340-5 Hamilton Teachers College Applications Register

AO RG 2-340-6 Hamilton Normal School Yearly Examination Registers

AO RG 2-340-7 Hamilton Normal School Final Examination Register

AO RG 2-340-8 Hamilton Normal School Training Registers Standard Courses

AO RG 2-340-9 Hamilton Teachers College Training Registers Special Courses

AO RG 2-340-10 Hamilton Normal School Student Record Cards

Hamilton Normal School. *Hamilton Normal School Memorial.* Hamilton, ON, *circa* 1920.

A register of the fallen from the school in the First World War. CIHM microfiche series, no. 88227.

Lakehead Teachers' College, 1960–1970s
Later the Faculty of Education, Lakehead University.

Yearbook
OHEC 1960/61–1968/69

Lakeshore Teachers' College, 1959–1975
In 1971 it was made part of York University, but closed in 1975.

Yearbook
OHEC 1959/60–1970/71

AO RG 2-269 Lakeshore Teachers' College Student Records, 1959–1971

AO RG 2-269-1 Lakeshore Teachers' College Student Records Cards

AO RG 2-269-2 Lakeshore Teachers' College Practice Teaching Registers

London Normal School, 1900–1973
In 1973, integrated with University of Western Ontario to form the Faculty of Education.

The Spectrum (yearbook)
OHEC 1935/36–1972/73 irregular holdings

Mnemosyne (yearbook)
CIHM microfiche series, no. P04543, vol. 1, no. 1, 1900

AORG 2-349 London Normal School Student Records, 1900–1973

    AO RG 2-349-1 London Normal School Admissions Register

    AO RG 2-349-2 London Normal School Examination Registers

    AO RG 2-349-3 London Normal School Training Registers

    AO RG 2-349-4 London Teachers' College Student Record Cards

AO RG 2-350 London Normal School Visitors Register, 1935–1951

University of Western Ontario Archives: Yearbooks, scrapbooks, photographs, correspondence, and other papers of the London Normal School, later London Teachers' College, now Faculty of Education, UWO, 1900–1985, and some early Department of Education material, 1870–1920.

EDUCATION AND ONTARIO FAMILY HISTORY

Laforest, J. F. *A Brief History of London Teachers' College.* Unpublished manuscript. University of Western Ontario Archives, 1959. B746.

Simmer, Marvin L. *The London Normal School and Rural Education in Southwestern Ontario.* London, ON: London & Middlesex Heritage Museum, 2009.

North Bay Normal School, 1909–1973

Integrated with Nipissing University College in 1973.

Yearbook
OHEC 1930/31–1972/73

AO RG 2-347 North Bay Normal School admissions register, 1909–1923

An Historical Sketch of N.B.N.S. — N.B.T.C.: 1905–1959. North Bay, ON: North Bay Teachers' College, *circa* 1959.

Dalziel, Graham G. *"Training Teachers for the North: The Early Development of Teacher Training in North Bay, Ont., 1905– 1920."* Master's thesis, University of Toronto, 1976.

Ontario College of Education

Pedantics (yearbook): The earlier years contain the students' literary works only, with no class photographs.

OHEC 1933–1967 irregular holdings: The OHEC collection includes a number of large, framed annual class group photographs for the Ontario College of Education and its successor institution.

OISE Library, OHEC Collection.

Executive Committee of the Literary Society, Faculty of Education, University of Toronto, 1907–1908, Easter Term.

University of Toronto Archives, A1974-0011, Ontario College of Education, 1907–1967: Among other material are found student records, consisting of ledgers containing examination results for the Faculty of Education (1907–1920) and the Ontario College of Education (1907–1955).

Inspiring Education, 1907–2007: Celebrating 100 Years of Studies in Education at the University of Toronto. Toronto: Ontario Institute for Studies in Education, University of Toronto, 2006.

Ottawa Normal School, 1875–1973

The Torch (yearbook)
OHEC 1929/30–1969/70

AO RG 2-368 Ottawa Normal School Student Records, 1875–1974. Online finding aid available.

Ottawa Normal School. Seventy-Fifth Anniversary, 1875–1950. Ottawa, ON: Alumni Association, 1950.

Desjarlais, Lionel. *History of the Faculty of Education of the University of Ottawa.* Ottawa, ON, 1998.

AO RG 2-256 Ottawa Model School student records, 1880–1939. Online finding aid available.

Peterborough Normal School, 1908–1973

Review (yearbook)
OHEC 1908/09–1970/71 irregular holdings: Peterborough Museum and Archives has holdings for 1921–1971.

AO RG 2-348 Peterborough Normal School Admissions Register, 1908–1923.

Queen's University Archives, Kingston. Peterborough Teachers College fonds 2229, 1908–1973: The fonds consists of sessional records, training registers, registration, and record cards.

St. Catharines Teachers' College, 1965–1971
In 1971 it became the College of Education at Brock University.

Compendium (yearbook)
OHEC 1965/66–1968/69

Moase, Reginald and McAuley, Donald. *25 Years of Teacher Education at Brock University.* St. Catharine's, ON: Vanwell Publishing, 1989.

Stratford Normal School, 1908–1973

The Classic (yearbook)
OHEC 1908/09–1971/72.
The Stratford Perth Archives has an almost complete run.

AO RG 2-254 Stratford Normal School Student Records, 1908–1972

> **AO RG 2-254-1** Stratford Normal School Entrance Registers

> **AO RG 2-254-2** Stratford Normal School Signature and Address Registers

> **AO RG 2-254-3** Stratford Normal School Admissions Register

> **AO RG 2-254-4** Stratford Normal School Sessional Registers

Coulter, J.W., and W.A.West, *A Short History of Stratford Teachers' College, 1908–1958*. Stratford, ON: *circa* 1958.
Gelman, Susan. "Stratford (Normal School) Teachers' College, 1908–1973." *Historical Studies in Education* 14 (2002), 113–20.

École normale de Sudbury, 1963–1974
In 1974, it became part of Laurentian University.

Annuaire (yearbook)
J.N. Desmarais Library, Laurentian University 1963/64–1971/72

L'Ecole normale de l'Université d'Ottawa, 1923–1969

It was founded in 1923 as the Ecole de pédagogie in 1923. In 1969 it was integrated into the Faculty of Education of the University of Ottawa.

Annuaire (yearbook)
OHEC 1939/40–1943/44; 1950/51–1968/69
University of Ottawa Archives 1933/34–1969/70

Toronto Normal School, 1847–1974

In 1974 it was absorbed into Ontario Teacher Education College. In 1979 this college was closed and became part of the University of Toronto.

Yearbook
OHEC 1912/13–1968/69 irregular holdings
1914 Internet Archive

AO RG 2-128 Toronto Normal School Student Records, 1847–1974

    AO RG 2-128-1 Toronto Normal School Admission Registers

    AO RG 2-128-2 Toronto Normal School Entrance Registers

    AO RG 2-128-3 Toronto Normal School Registers of Students' Local Addresses

    AO RG 2-128-4 Toronto Normal School Examination Registers

AO RG 2-128-5 Toronto Normal School Practice Teaching Registers

AO RG 2-128-6 Toronto Normal School Teacher Certification Registers

AO RG 2-128-7 Toronto Teachers' College Student Record Cards

Ontario Department of Public Instruction. *The Normal School for Ontario: Its Design and Functions: Chiefly Taken from the Report of the Chief Superintendent of Education for Ontario, for the Year 1869.* Toronto: Hunter, Rose, 1871. CIHM microfiche series, no. 62320. The material has mostly been taken from the report of the chief superintendent for 1869, but lists of students are included, along with a section on the history of normal schools.

From Cradle to Computer: A History of St. James Square, the Birthplace of Ontario Education. Toronto: Ryerson Polytechnic Institute, 1984.

Prentice, Alison. "Like Friendly Atoms in Chemistry? Women and Men at Normal School in Mid-Nineteenth-Century Toronto." in *Old Ontario: Essays in Honour of J.M.S. Careless,* edited by David Keane and Colin Read. Toronto: Dundurn Press, 1990.

Sage, W.N. *Toronto Normal School, 1847–1947.* Toronto, 1947.

Toronto Normal School Jubilee Celebration (October 31st, November 1st and 2nd, 1897): Biographical Sketches and Names of Successful Students 1847 to 1875. Toronto: Warwick Bro's & Rutter, 1898. CIHM microfiche series, no. 24939.

Toronto Normal School, 1847–1947. Toronto: School of Graphic Arts, 1947. Internet Archive.

Windsor Teachers' College, 1962–1970
In 1970 it became part of the University of Windsor.

Magister (yearbook)
OHEC 1962/63–1969/70

Records Covering More Than One School

AO RG 2-129 Normal Schools Historical Files, 1851–1917. Miscellaneous materials on Ontario's normal schools.

AO RG 2-257 Ontario Teachers' Colleges Historical Files, *circa* 1850–1973. A miscellaneous collection of material relating to the various teachers' colleges in Ontario, but focusing primarily on the Toronto Teachers' College.

AO RG 2-329 Normal and Model School Examination Papers, 1859–1896. Pre-printed examination papers for students of normal and model schools in Ontario, specifically the Toronto Normal and Model Schools, 1859–1879; Goderich Model School, 1879; county model schools, 1884; and the Ontario School of Pedagogy, 1894–1896.

AO RG 2-355 F.W. Merchant's Normal Schools Inspection Reports, 1914–1915. Inspection reports made by F.W. Merchant, inspector of normal schools, on the normal schools of Toronto, Hamilton, North Bay, London, Ottawa, Peterborough, and Stratford.

AO RG 2-357 Ontario Normal College Student Records, 1895–1905

AO RG 2-357-1 Ontario Normal College Applications Register

AO RG 2-357-2 Ontario Normal School Examination Records

AO RG 2-360 Model Schools Student Teachers Registers, 1908–1914. Information about student teachers who attended model schools in Ontario (with the exception of the Toronto and Ottawa model schools).

AO RG 2-361 Normal Schools Application Records, 1869–1921. The applications dated 1869–1872 are for the Toronto Normal School; those for 1897–1921 also include Ottawa, London, Hamilton, Peterborough, Stratford, and North Bay schools.

AO RG 2-374 Faculties of Education Final Examination Reports, 1906–1912. One register only that records the results of the final examinations held at the Faculties of Education at Queen's University and the University of Toronto for First Class Teachers' Certificates.

Past Principals of Ontario Normal Schools, January, 1905. CIHM microfiche series, no. 77333.

Further Reading

Althouse, J.G. "The Ontario Teacher: A Historical Account of Progress, 1800–1910." Doctor of Pedagogy dissertation, University of Toronto, 1929. Toronto: Ontario Teachers' Federation, 1967.

Fiorino, Albert. *Teacher Education in Ontario: A History, 1843–1976.* Toronto: Commission on Declining School Enrolments in Ontario (CODE), 1978.

TEACHERS' ORGANIZATIONS

Voluntary associations of teachers began as early as 1851, as in that year and the one following, mention can be found of the Dumfries Teachers' Association and similar associations in Northumberland, Durham, Huron, and Welland in the *Documentary History of Education* and other educational periodicals. The *Journal of Education*, through the 1860s and 1870s, records teachers' associations in the following counties: York, Oxford, Prince Edward, Elgin, Grenville, Northumberland, Bruce, Middlesex, Huron, and Wentworth, as well as in northern Ontario.

By the 1860s there was a belief among teachers that a province-wide organization was needed to forward their goals for the profession. In 1861, the Teachers' Association of Canada West was formed, later to be called the Teachers' Association of Canada and then the Ontario Teachers' Association. In 1892, this association and several others united under the title of the Ontario Educational Association (OEA).

One of the greatest achievements of the teachers' organizations was the province-wide pension scheme that came into existence in 1917. The earlier attempt at superannuation for "old and wornout teachers" had been perceived as charity and, in any case, the amounts awarded were woefully inadequate. The OEA ceased to exist in 1986.

After the First World War, there was a need perceived for organizations that could advocate on behalf of teachers for working conditions, tenure, and salaries. The first group to organize was the Federation of Women Teachers' Associations, formed in 1918. It was followed by the Ontario Secondary School Teachers' Federation in 1919, and the Ontario Public School Men Teachers' Federation in 1921. The Teaching Profession Act of 1944 brought the Ontario Teachers' Federation into existence to represent all teachers in the province, and in 1997, teachers were granted their own regulatory body with the establishment of the Ontario College of Teachers.

The Ontario teachers' organizations that exist today typically do not have records that are accessible to the public. The exception is the Ontario College of Teachers' "Find a Teacher" database (*www.otffeo.on.ca*), the College's public register, which lists everyone who has been certified to teach in Ontario's publicly funded schools. But note that deceased teachers are not part of this database.

Why, then, should you be interested in teacher organizations' histories and publications? Because both are a great way of seeing how the profession has changed over the years, especially with regard to such major issues as salaries and working conditions. The histories also have lists of names and photographs of officers and an ancestor may well have been involved in one or more of these organizations.

List of Organizations

Elementary Teachers Federation of Ontario (ETFO)
480 University Avenue, Suite 1000
Toronto, Ontario, Canada M5G 1V2
www.etfo.org

An amalgamation of the Ontario Public School Teachers' Federation (formerly the Ontario Public School Men Teachers'

Federation) and the Federation of Women Teachers' Associations
of Ontario.

Ontario Secondary School Teachers Federation (OSSTF)
60 Mobile Drive
Toronto, Ontario, Canada M4A 2P3
www.osstf.on.ca

Ontario English Catholic Teachers' Association (OECTA)
65 St. Clair Avenue West
Toronto, Ontario, Canada M4T 2Y8
www.oecta.on.ca

Ontario Teachers' Federation
1300 Yonge Street, Suite 200
Toronto, Ontario, Canada M4T 1X3
www.otffeo.on.ca

Ontario College of Teachers (OCT)
121 Bloor Street East
Toronto, Ontario, Canada M4W 3M5
www.oct.ca

Retired Teachers of Ontario
18 Spadina Road, Suite 300
Toronto, Ontario, Canada M5R 2S7
www.rto-ero.org

Record Sources for the Teachers' Organizations

York University Archives F0181 Federation of Women
Teachers' Associations of Ontario fonds, 1918–1998. The entire

set of records of the organization was donated to York University when the organization ceased to exist in 1998.

York University Archives F0532 Rendezvous Club fonds, 1937–2004. The Rendezvous Club of Toronto was formed in 1937 by the Social Group of Retired Women Teachers as a way for members to maintain friendships made during the teaching years, through social activities, and also to support the work of the Ontario Association of Superannuated Women Teachers in maintaining adequate pensions for retired teachers.

York University Archives F0196 Retired Women Teachers of Ontario fonds.

AO F1209 Ontario Educational Association fonds, 1860–1946. *Ontario Educational Association: Jubilee Banquet, Convocation Hall, University of Toronto, April 18, 1911.* Toronto, 1911. Includes index of those present at the banquet. Internet Archive CIHM microfiche series, no. 78188.

Ontario Educational Association. *Yearbook and Proceedings.* Toronto: The Association, 1865–1960. Selected years available at the Internet Archive.

Publications of the Teachers' Organizations

Federation of Women Teachers' Associations of Ontario and Ontario Public School Men Teachers' Federation. *The Educational Courier,* 1930–1979.
Federation of Women Teachers' Associations of Ontario. *Bulletin,* 1924–1930.
Ontario Public School Men Teachers' Federation. *The Advance,*

circa 1922–1930.

Ontario Secondary School Teachers Federation. *Bulletin, circa* 1920.

Further Reading

Hardy, John H. "Teachers' Organizations in Ontario: An Historical Account of Their Part in Ontario Educational Development and Their Influence on the Teacher and Teaching, 1840–1938." Doctor of Pedagogy dissertation. University of Toronto, 1938.

Hopkins, R.A. *The Long March: A History of the Ontario Public School Men Teachers' Federation.* Toronto: Baxter, 1969.

Johnston, Harriett, Jessie P. Semple, and A.A. Gray. *The Story of the Women Teachers' Association of Toronto.* Vol. 1: 1892–1930. Toronto: T. Nelson, 1930.

OTF at 20: Recollections of the First Two Decades of the Ontario Teachers' Federation. Toronto: Ontario Teachers' Federation, 1964.

Robinson, Stephen G.B. *Do Not Erase: The Story of OSSTF.* Toronto: Ontario Secondary School Teachers' Federation, 1971.

Shackleton, Doris French. *High Button Bootstraps: Federation of Women Teachers' Associations of Ontario, 1918–1968.* Toronto: Ryerson Press, 1968.

Staton, P. A. *Speak with Their Own Voices: A Documentary History of the Federation of Women Teachers' Associations of Ontario and the Women Elementary Public School Teachers of Ontario.* Toronto: Federation of Women Teachers' Associations of Ontario, 1987.

Walker, Eva K. *The Story of the Women Teachers' Association of Toronto.* Vol. 2: 1931–1963. Toronto: Copp, Clark, 1963.

INSPECTORATE—RENFREW, NORTH. Inspector—E. T. White, B.A., B. Paed. Pembroke.

Renfrew, North; Town of Pembroke; Village of Cobden.

Classification of certificates:—

	I.	II.	III.	T.	D.	K.	Totals.
Men,	0	4	1	2	1	0	8
Women,	2	22	37	9	18	1	89

No. Schools. Rural—71 Urban—4

Name of School. (In the case of rural schools the township and the number of section is given; in cities, towns and villages the name of the municipality.)		Secretary of the Board.	Post Office of Section.	Name of Teacher.	Certificate.	Salary.	Assessment of Section.	Cont. or V class.	Kind of Building.	Value of School Property.	Value of Equipment.	Average Attendance.
Algona, N., & Hagarty.	U1	Pierce, Arthur	Deacon	Bulger, Annie	T	300	33,260		F	900	24	13
Algona, South	1	Roche, Michael	Cormac	Galvin, Margaret	III	400	41,000		F	900	73	15
Algona, S., & Grattan.	U3	Neitzel, Amlel.	Eganville	Dwyer, Margaret	D	325	65,067		F	500	37	30
Algona, South	4	Rankins, Patrick	Ruby	Fitzgerald, Agnes	D	325	65,476		F	800	35	11
do	6	Michaelis, Geo.	Augsburg	Dooner, Margaret	T	300	26,520	V	F	700	21	7
Alice, Stafford and Petawawa	U1	Buder, John	Pembroke	O'Connor, Lorina	III	500	164,000		B	2,800	39	30
Alice and Stafford	2	O'Meara, Wm. H.	Pembroke	Agnew, Gertrude	III	500	125,000		B	1,200	48	17
Alice and Stafford	U3	Walford, H. S.	Locksley	Gunter, Lennox	III	450	135,000		B	1,700	12	36
Alice	4	Davis, Robt. H.	Davis Mills	Cahill, Malvinia	III	425	70,000		F	1,000	35	19
Alice	5	Schultz, H. E.	Pembroke	Zieroth, Selma	D	450	66,925		F	850	33	24
Alice	6	Kennedy, Edwin	Forestlea	O'Meara, Annie	II	450	68,500		B	2,100	49	22
Alice and Stafford	U7	Meltz, Wm.	Locksley Station	Cully, Mary C.	II	450	72,020		F	700	69	11
Alice	8	Mebs, Henry	Alice	Chaput, Rose	III	350	38,000		L	900	69	16
Bromley	8	Petznick, Gustav	Woito	Sullivan, Annie	III	350	18,300	V	B	700	43	11
do	9	Reynolds, B. J.	Osceola (R.M.D.)	Powers, Katie	III	395	132,000		B	600	38	26
do	3	McDiarmid, Geo.	Cobden (R.M.D.)	Cole, Katie B.	D	450	135,000		B	1,475	68	15
do	5	Kerr, John	Douglas	Boland, Fannie	III	625	162,000		B	2,000	62	54
do	7	Patterson, Johnson.	Douglas (R.M.D.)	Montgomery, Sara.	I	500			F	3,500	85	
do	8	Foley, Hugh	Pine Valley	Dalglish, Annie	I	500	256,000		B	1,300	90	19
Buchanan	9	McCarthy, Florence.	Wylie	O'Gorman, Elizabeth (Summer School)	D		130,000	V	F	900	83	18
do	2	Cuthbert, Wm.	Chalk River	Fraser, Barbara	II	600	19,673		L	250	9	3
do	3			Mulligan, Sadie	III	425	133,600		F	1,800	66	65
Head	1	Dunlop, W. P.	Mackeys	Conway, Margaret.	T	300	30,600		F	850	30	16

The "Blue Books" or Schools and Teachers in the Province of Ontario. Toronto: Ontario Department of Education, 1913.

APPENDIX G.—*SUPERANNUATED TEACHERS,TEACHERS WITHDRAWING FROM THE FUND.*

1. SUPERANNUATED TEACHERS.

(CONTINUED FROM LAST REPORT).

Allowances granted during 1886.

No.	NAME.	Age.	Year of Teaching in Ontario.	Amount of Superannuation Allowance.
				$ c.
774	Daniel Wright	74	18	108 00
775	Ellen Bowes	51	21½	129 00
776	William Boal	33	10	66 50
777	William Noble	51	22½	135 00
778	Alex. T. Rothwell	54	20½	129 00
779	Roderick Ferguson	56	30	180 00
780	James McGurn	50	32	205 50
781	Charles Shortt	64	24½	168 50
782	Samuel Joyce	64	22	152 00
783	Chas. MacKinnon	61	19	114 00
784	Stephen Henry Leighton	51	21	146 00
785	Clara Louisa Brown	39	13	90 00
786	Edwin W. Pillar	60	30	193 00
787	Stephen B. Cameron	62	35	210 00
788	J. W. Bingham	50	26½	175 00
789	Samuel Rothwell	61	24	164 00
790	Jeremiah George House	62	37	246 00
791	Wm. H. Bly	60	27	184 00
792	Eli Masales	60	34	225 00
793	Jno. Drummond	59	32	201 00
794	Jno. Clarke	67	8½	51 00
795-397	Jno. Mitchell	58	21½	147 50
796	Jno. Parke	60	34½	235 50
379	James Hodgson	75	33½	234 50
797	Alex. T. Leitch	47	19	130 00
798	Jno. N. Dochstader	46	23	138 00
799	Jas. McLean	39	13½	93 50
800	*Gilbert French	50	24½	155 50

* First payment to commence with January, 1887.

Annual Report, Ontario Department of Education, 1886.

Record Sources for Teachers and Teaching

Archives of Ontario RG 2

RG 2-17 Education Office Annual Reports of Local Superintendents and Local Boards of Trustees, 1850–1870. One section of these reports gives the names, salaries, religion, experience, and qualifications of the teachers. Available on microfilm. Online finding aid available.

RG 2-18 Department of Public Instruction Local Treasurers' Annual Reports, 1852–1872. These financial reports include the names of teachers and the salary amounts paid. Online finding aid available.

RG 2-20 County Grammar School Inspectors' Reports, 1855–1871. These reports include information on the qualifications and the standard of work of teachers. Online finding aid available

RG 2-28 Records of Proceedings of the Committee of Examiners of Candidates for Masterships of County Grammar Schools.

RG 2-37 Department of Education Files Regarding Investigations, Disputes, and Arbitrations, 1874–1896. Concerns and investigations into the conduct and morality of teachers are included. Online finding aid available.

RG 2-47 Department of Education Personnel Records, 1844–1882. Appointments, salaries, religious denominations, and resignations of Department of Public Instruction and Department of Education personnel (including normal and model schools), 1844–1882.

RG 2-87 Department of Education Local School Histories and Teaching Experiences Files, 1846–1896. Documents the teaching experiences of some nineteenth-century Ontario teachers and the early history of schools in some towns and townships in the province. Available on microfilm. Online finding aid available.

As part of the work of compiling his monumental *Documentary History of Education in Upper Canada*, John George Hodgins requested teachers throughout Ontario to send him accounts of their personal experience and the histories of their local schools. Their responses are to be found in these files. There are additional accounts of teaching and school histories in **Fonds F 1207**, the John G. Hodgins fonds.

RG 2-98 Algoma Public School Inspectorate Records, 1862–1868, 1875–1888, 1903–1935. As part of the records created or obtained by public school inspectors carrying out their duties, there are included lists of school teachers, applications for teacher certificates, and reports regarding particular schools.

RG 2-100 Annual Reports of Public School Inspectors, 1912–1937. Included in the annual reports of schools throughout Ontario is information such as the names and qualifications of teaching staffs, and the quality of work done by teachers and students.

RG 2-100-1 Public School Inspectors' Annual Reports for Halton County No. 4 and Wentworth County No. 2 Inspectorate, 1912–1937.

RG 2-100-2 Public School Inspectors' Annual Reports for Timiskaming District No. 1 Inspectorate, 1927–1933.

RG 2-100-3 Public School Inspectors' Annual Reports for Cochrane District No. 1 Inspectorate, 1913–1935.

RG 2-100-4 Public School Inspectors' Annual Reports for Timiskaming District No. 2 Inspectorate, 1918–1927.

RG 2-100-5 Public School Inspectors' Annual Reports for Sullivan Township, 1931–1933.

RG 2-100-6 Public School Inspectors' Annual Reports for Frontenac County No. 1 and Lennox and Addington County No. 1 Inspectorate, 1912–1926, 1932.

RG 2-100-7 Public School Inspectors' Annual Reports for Ontario County No. 4 Inspectorate, 1914–1933.

RG 2-100-8 Public School Inspectors' Annual Reports for Manitoulin District No. 1 Inspectorate, 1928–1933.

RG 2-101 Roman Catholic Separate School Inspectors' Reports, 1882–1933.

RG 2-105 High School Inspectors' Annual Reports, 1872–1883, 1885–1932. Included in the annual reports of inspections carried out in high schools are the names and qualifications of teaching staff and the quality of work of teachers and students. See also, RG 2-106 High School and Collegiate Institute Inspectors' Field Notes, 1917–1944, 1949–1953. Online finding aid available.

RG 2-107 High School Correspondence Files, 1871–1898. Correspondence between the Department of Education and high-school trustees, inspectors, principals, as well as municipalities and the general public. Among the subjects discussed are the teaching staffs of various schools. Online finding aid available.

RG 2-108 Continuation School Inspectors' Reports, 1906–1913, 1918, 1924. Included in these reports are the names and qualifications of teachers and the quality of work done by teachers and students.

RG 2-110 Teachers' Superannuation Financial Records, 1854–1948. Financial registers and other records that record the contributions made to and payments from the superannuation fund first established for Ontario teachers in 1853.

RG 2-110-1 Teachers' Superannuation Subscription Books, 1854–1885.

RG 2-110-2 Teachers' Superannuation Pay Lists, 1856–1945.

RG 2-110-3 Register of Compassionate Allowance to Teachers and Inspectors, 1920–1948.

RG 2-110-4 Teachers' Superannuation Cash Book, 1920–1921.

RG 2-114 Teacher Superannuation Files, 1820–1919. These are the applications for payment from the teachers' (and later school inspectors') superannuation fund, along with related documents, schedules of pension applications, and lists of superannuated teachers. Available on microfilm.

RG 2-114-1 Teacher Superannuation Application Files, 1820–1876. An online finding aid, indexed by name, available.

RG 2-114-2 Schedule of Teacher Pension Applications, 1858–1877.

RG 2-114-3 Lists of Superannuated Teachers, 1876–1879, 1885.

RG 2-142 County Boards of Education Records, 1850–1910. Consists primarily of minutes of the county boards of education (examiners), a body established under the Common Schools Act of 1850 to examine teachers' qualifications and either issue or cancel County Common School Teachers' Certificates. Available on microfilm. Online finding aid available.

RG 2-144 Public School Inspectors' Reports and Correspondence Files, 1870–1908. Reports in this series include inspectors' reports on Third Class teachers, lists of teachers, and inspectors' certificates regarding teachers' work and salaries. Online finding aid available.

RG 2-184 Lists of High School Principals and Assistants, 1891. Forms submitted by high-school principals listing the names, degree, university attended, salary, date of certificate, and date of appointment of high-school principals and assistants.

RG 2-208 Public School Inspectors' Operational Files, 1884–1965, lacking 1885–1898 and 1905–1943. Series consists of the operational files of some public-school inspectors. Files may include correspondence, petitions for the creation of new school sections in unorganized townships, minutes of school meetings, information bulletins, and copies of departmental regulations.

RG 2-246 Northwestern Ontario Dissolved School Board Files, 1848–1997. The series consists of administrative and operational records of dissolved and discontinued school boards in the Kenora, Rainy River, and Thunder Bay districts, and the Patricia Portion of northwestern Ontario, and contains some teacher and employee records.

RG 2-248 Ottawa Valley Region Dissolved School Board Records, 1871–1985. The series consists of administrative and operational records of dissolved and discontinued school boards in the counties of Carleton, Grenville, Lanark, Prescott, Renfrew, Russell, and Stormont, Dundas, and Glengarry, and contains some teacher and employee records.

RG 2-273 Continuation School Inspectors' Field Notes, 1921–1944, lacking 1937. Field notes contain the inspectors' observations on school conditions and qualifications and work of teachers.

RG 2-275 Northeastern Ontario Dissolved School Boards Records, 1908–1983, 1987–1994. The series consists of administrative and operational records of dissolved and discontinued school boards in Cochrane, Nipissing, and Timiskaming districts and contains some teacher and employee records.

RG 2-277 Mid-northern Ontario dissolved school boards records, 1912–1994. The series consists of administrative and operational records of dissolved and discontinued school boards in Algoma, Manitoulin, and Sudbury districts, and the Regional Municipality of Sudbury, and contains some teacher and employee records.

RG 2-301 Registers of First and Second Class Teachers' Certificates, 1853–1972. Record the granting of First and Second Class Teachers' Certificates by the Department of Education.

RG 2-301-1 Registers of Permanent First and Second Class Teachers' Certificates, 1853–1969.

RG 2-301-2 Registers of Interim First and Second Class Public School Teachers' Certificates, 1908–1972.

RG 2-317 Registers of Third Class Teachers' Certificates, 1877–1948. Record the granting of Third Class Teachers' Certificates and any applications for renewals or extensions. Online finding aid available.

RG 2-318 Registers of Head Masters, Principals, Assistant Head Masters, Vice-Principals, and Permanent High School Specialists Certificates, 1875–1969. Record the granting of certificates to those who qualified for permanent certificates for the positions of principal or headmaster, vice-principal or assistant headmaster, as well as High School Assistants' Certificates and High School Specialists' Certificates. Online finding aid available.

RG 2-319 Registers of Interim High School Teachers' Certificates, 1889–1969. Record the granting of Interim High School Certificates, including both High School Assistants' Certificates and High School Specialists' Certificates. Online finding aid available.

RG 2-320 First Class Teachers' Certificates examination applications, 1881–1884. Applications submitted by teachers who wished to write the examinations in order to qualify for First Class Teachers' Certificates.

RG 2-321 Toronto Model School Student Records, 1853–1938.

RG 2-321-1 Toronto Model School Daily Attendance Registers.

RG 2-321-2 Toronto Model School Student Fee Register.

RG 2-321-3 Toronto Model School Class Lists of Male Students.

RG 2-322-4 Toronto Model School Admissions Register of Male Students.

RG 2-324 Interim and permanent kindergarten and elementary school teachers certificate registers, 1909–1968. Record the granting of certificates to those qualified for Interim and Permanent Kindergarten Assistants', Kindergarten Directors', Kindergarten-Primary, and Primary School Specialists' Teachers' Certificates. Online finding aid available.

RG 2-325 Temporary Teachers' Certificates Registers, 1885–1962. Record the granting of temporary teachers' certificates, made necessary periodically, because of teacher shortages.

RG 2-325-1 Registers of Temporary Teachers' Certificates for Students of Toronto or Ottawa Normal Schools, 1885–1946.

RG 2-325-2 Registers of Temporary Teachers' Certificates for High Schools, Continuation Schools and Special Public School, 1922–1947.

RG 2-325-3 Summer Course Temporary Teachers' Certificates Register, 1947–1952, 1954.

RG 2-325-4 In-Service Training Program Teachers' Certificates Registers, 1952–1960.

RG 2-325-5 Registers of Ontario College of Education Special Summer Course Interim High School Teachers' Certificates, 1955–1962.

RG 2-326 Special Subjects Teachers' Certificates Registers, 1883–1965. Record the granting of teachers' certificates, intermediate certificates, and supervisors' certificates.

RG 2-326-1 Art Teachers' Certificates Register, 1883–1887.

RG 2-326-2 Household Science Teachers' Certificates Registers, 1897–1965.

RG 2-326-3 Elementary Teachers' Special Subject Certificate Registers, 1909–1963.

RG 2-326-4 Interim High School Specialists' Certificate Registers, 1913–1963.

RG 2-326-5 Intermediate and Supervisors' Special Subject Certificate Registers, 1912–1965.

RG 2-327 County Model School Inspectors Reports, 1877–1903. Information in these reports includes submissions on the principal and faculty of the model school being inspected. Online finding aid available.

RG 2-328 Teachers' Institutes Meeting Records, 1909–1931. These records consist of two registers recording meetings of teachers' institutes in Ontario, which provided a forum for teachers to discuss professional issues. Listed are the dates of meetings, names of speakers, and topics discussed.

RG 2-330 Registers of Manual Training Teachers' Certificates, 1904–1971. Record the granting of certificates to individuals who had completed the required course for teaching manual training.

RG 2-333 Teachers of Religious and Educational Communities Registers, 1907–1909. Records information about members of religious and educational communities who participated in summer courses in order to upgrade existing teacher qualifications.

RG 2-334 Inspectors' and Examiners' Certificate Registers, 1871–1979. Four registers that record the granting of school inspectors' or examiners' certificates. The first volume, 1871–1927, lists names and personal details; the second and third volumes, 1871–1901, contain names only. The fourth volume, 1902–1979, records the granting of Public School Inspectors' Certificates. Online finding aid available.

RG 2-335 Kindergarten Teachers' Certificate Examination Registers, 1887–1918. Record of the results of examinations taken by students seeking to qualify for a Kindergarten Assistants' Certificate, a Kindergarten Directors' Certificate, or a Kindergarten-Primary Certificate. Online finding aid available.

RG 2-342 Departmental Reports of the Final Examinations of Teachers in Training, 1877–1962. Record of the final examination marks obtained by students of normal schools throughout Ontario who were seeking a teachers' certificate from the Department of Education. Online finding aid available.

RG 2-362 Toronto Model School Visitors Register, 1853–1885.

RG 2-371 Special Teaching Subjects Examination Reports, 1887; 1897–1930. Record of the results of examinations taken by students wishing to qualify for teachers' certificates in art, commercial course, domestic science, or music. Online finding aid available.

Teachers and Inspectors' Examinations

Teachers were required to pass a series of examinations to qualify for the various levels of teaching certificate available. The OHEC collection has a selection of the examination papers that were administered to teachers and those who wished to become school inspectors:

Examinations of Public School Teachers
1st Class Provincial Certificates
2nd Class Provincial Certificates
3rd Class County Certificates
First and Second Class Professional Examinations, Normal School
Elementary School Inspectors' Examinations

Published Lists of Teachers

"List of Teachers in the Home District in 1820–1822." In *Documentary History of Education in Upper Canada*, vol. 1, edited by J. George Hodgins. Toronto: Warwick Bros & Rutter, 1894: 183. Consult the volumes of this documentary history for the names of teachers in other contexts which appear throughout.

The *Journals of the Legislative Assembly of Upper Canada* are discussed fully as a source for educational history in Roy Reynolds, *A Guide to Published Government Documents Relating to Education in Ontario*. Here Reynolds records the lists of the names of grammar-school masters in the *Appendix on Public Accounts* from 1825 through to most of the years of the 1840s. The names of many of the teachers in the common schools are recorded in the *Appendices* to these journals from 1828 to 1840.

"Local Superintendents of Schools in the Several Municipalities of Upper Canada" [title varies]. In *Annual Report of the Minister of Education*, 1851 to 1891.

"The Grammar Schools of Upper Canada." In *Annual Report of the Minister of Education*, 1856; 1858–1859; 1861. The names of headmasters and their qualifications are listed.

"Lists of Provincial Certificates Granted by the Education Department" [title varies]. In *Annual Report of the Minister of Education*, 1855 and most years following. This list was published until at least 1918, with the result that when used in conjunction with Public and Separate Schools and Teachers in the Province of Ontario, most Ontario teachers can be tracked throughout their careers.

"List of Normal School Students Who Hold Legal Certificates of Qualification Now Valid Throughout Ontario." In *The Normal School for Ontario: Its Design and Functions: Chiefly Taken from the Report of the Chief Superintendent of Education for Ontario, for the Year 1869,* Toronto: Hunter, Rose, 1871: 42–58.

"Names of Persons Who Have Received Certificates and Who Are Eligible To Be Appointed Public School Inspectors in Any

County, City or Town in Ontario." In *Annual Report of the Minister of Education*, 1872.

"List of Public School Inspectors." In *Annual Report of the Minister of Education*, 1872; 1901; 1903.

"Statement in Detail of the Superannuated Common School Teachers in Upper Canada…, With the Pensions Paid." [title varies]. In *Annual Reports of the Minister of Education*, 1854–present.

> Wm. M. Hynes. Religion: Presbyterian. Birth: Ireland. Residence: Brockville. Cause of Discontinuing Teaching: Age & Debility. Age in 1856: 62. Years of Teaching in U.C.: 34. Subscription: 1.0.0. Pension: 25.10.0. Abstract of case: Commenced in 1818 and taught in the County of Leeds 34 years. *Annual Report of the Minister of Education*, 1855.

"Reminiscences of Superannuated Teachers." In *Documentary History of Education in Upper Canada, 1791–1876*, edited by J. George Hodgins, Toronto: King's Printer, 1894–1910, vol. 4, 146–53; vol. 5, 271–87; vol. 8, 297–304; vol. 9, 295–303; vol. 28, 241–84.

"Names of Persons Who have Received High School Head Masters' Certificates Since 1875." In *Annual Report of the Minister of Education*, 1890.

"Names of Persons Who Have Qualified as High School Assistants." In *Annual Report of the Minister of Education*, 1890.

"List of Head Masters and Assistants of High Schools (Including Collegiate Institutes)" [title varies]. In *Annual Report of the Minister of Education,* 1890, 1897, 1918.

Public and Separate Schools and Teachers in the Province of Ontario. (Variously known as *Schools and Teachers in the Province of Ontario* and *The Blue Books*) Toronto: King's Printer, 1911–1966. These lists, published by the Department of Education, are the primary source for information on teachers in the first half of the twentieth century. They contain an astonishing amount of detail, including qualifications, home addresses, and salaries for each teacher. The OHEC collection has a complete run. The years 1911 to 1922 are available on the Internet Archive.

"List of Inspectors." In *The Township School Area in Ontario,* Ontario Department of Education, Toronto: King's Printer, 1948: 12–24. Toronto Board of Education. *Handbook.* Toronto: The Board, 1915–1954. Contains lists of teachers by school, with subject taught, rank in the school, qualifications, years of service in Toronto, total years of teaching, and salary.

War Memorials, Rolls of Honour, and Commemorative Plaques

Many schools have war memorials and other kinds of plaques on their walls, commemorating former principals, teachers, and students. It may be necessary to contact an individual school to find out if it has such a memorial. To obtain school contact information, visit the Ontario Ministry of Education's "School Information Finder" (*www.edu.gov.on.ca/eng/sift*). These memorials may also have been transcribed by the local branch of the Ontario Genealogical Society (OGS). To contact OGS

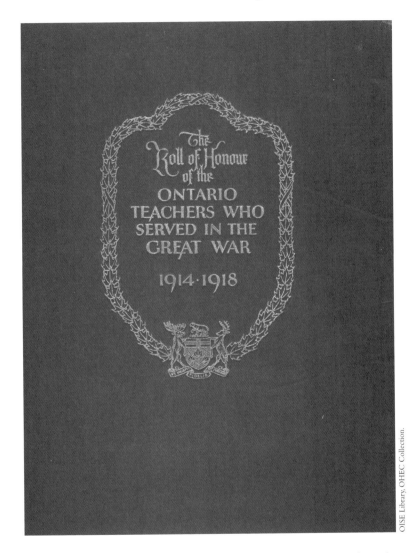

Cover of the Roll of Honour of Ontario Teachers Who Served in the Great War, 1914–1918. Toronto: Ryerson Press, 1922.

branches, visit the relevant section of the OGS website (*www.ogs. on.ca/branches.php*).

One such OGS initiative underway is the Toronto Branch "For King and Country" project. A volunteer is digitally photographing and transcribing all the war memorials and commemorative plaques in the schools of the Toronto District School Board. As they are completed, transcriptions will appear online in a searchable database (*torontofamilyhistory.org/ kingandcountry*).

For some idea of the scale of information available on war memorials, at the time of writing this the project had completed work in forty-nine schools finding a total of 20,133 names.

"Teachers Who Have Enlisted for Overseas Service." *Annual Report of the Minister of Education, 1915."*

The Roll of Honour of Ontario Teachers Who Served in the Great War 1914–1918. Toronto: Ryerson Press, 1922.

Teachers' Biographies, Memoirs, and Personal Recollections

Beattie, Susan M. "Common School Teachers in Nineteenth-Century Ontario: The Correspondence of Moses Albert James, 1868–1877." Master's thesis, University of Toronto, 1993. Moses James worked as common school teacher in Durham County from 1868 to 1878. He corresponded with family, school fields, and colleagues describing the life and concerns of teachers of the time. The original correspondence is housed in the Baldwin Room, Toronto Reference Library, Toronto.

Campbell, Helen Richards. *From Chalkdust to Hayseed.* Belleville, ON: Mika Publishers, 1975.

Chalk, Challenge and Change: Stories from Women Teachers in Ontario, 1920–1979. Oakville, ON: BEL Learning

Publications, 2006. As told by members of the Retired Teachers of Ontario.

Clement, Andrew D. *The Bell and the Book*. Cobalt, ON: Highway Book Shop, 1987.

Devine, Marjorie. *Irma*. Toronto: Vauve Press, 2002.

Disbrowe, Harold B. *A Schoolman's Odyssey*. London, ON: Faculty of Education, University of Western Ontario, 1984.

Fair, Myrtle. *I Remember the One-Room School*. Cheltenham, ON: Boston Mills Press, 1979.

Field, John L. *Janet Carnochan*. Markham, ON: Fitzhenry & Whiteside, 1985.

Gray, John Morgan. *A. W. Mackenzie, M.A., D.D., The Grove, Lakefield: A Memoir*. Toronto: Grove Old Boys' Association, 1938.

Hay, Gordon C. *Those Were the Days: The Ontario Secondary School, 1945–1970*. London, ON: Third Eye, 1988.

Killan, Gerald. *David Boyle: From Artisan to Archaeologist*. Toronto: University of Toronto Press, 1983.

Lamont, Graham. *These Beads of Coloured Days: An Ode to Life in Rural Schools*. 2006.

Laycock, John A. *Fifty Years in Huntsville*. Huntsville, ON: Friends of Muskoka Pioneer Museum, 1996.

Leonard, Wilbur. *The Tune of the Hickory Stick: Tales of a Backwoods Teacher*. Owen Sound, ON: Stan Brown Printers, 1988.

Ludgate, Marjorie Holley. *Walk Up the Creek*. Ste-Anne-de-Bellevue, QC: Shoreline, *circa* 2001.

McKague, Andrew Hill. *From Farm Lad to Educator*. Erin, ON: Boston Mills Press, 1989.

Moments in Time: A Collection of the Moments Remembered by East York Women Teachers. Toronto: East York Women Teachers' Association, 1993.

Morgan, D. *Chalkdust in My Blood*. Cornwall, ON: Vesta Publications, 1975.

Petrone, Penny. *Schoolmarm*. Thunder Bay, ON: Thunder Bay Historical Museum, 2007.

Robertson, Jessie E. *A Teacher's Life: Jessie E. Robertson; With Extracts from Diaries, Essays and Letters*, by her sisters and friends. Hamilton, ON: Griffin & Kidner, 1890. ECO CIHM microfiche series, no. 93645.

Rupnow, Mavis, and Elaner Pound. *Forever Young: Retired Women Teachers of Ontario, Belleville Branch*. Belleville, ON: Epic Press, *circa* 2005.

Shaw, Bertha M.C. *Broken Threads: Memories of a Northern Ontario Schoolteacher*. New York: Exposition Press, 1955.

Shaw, Bertha M.C. *Laughter and Tears*. New York: Exposition Press, 1957. The experiences of a teacher in early-twentieth-century Owen Sound.

Stabler, Ernest. *Rose McQueen and Stratford*. N.p.: *circa* 1985.

Whiting, Ruth. *Not a Proper Schoolmarm?* Oakland, ON: self-published, 1989.

CHAPTER 5

Curriculum and Textbooks

CURRICULUM IN ONTARIO

It was not until 1844, when Egerton Ryerson became Assistant Superintendent of Education, that an effort was made to establish a standard curriculum for Ontario pupils. For more than thirty years his views would dictate the direction that schooling would take in Ontario. Ryerson's first year as Assistant Superintendent was spent travelling in the United States and Europe to view systems of education elsewhere. In Ireland, he was impressed by the system of national textbooks and it was the Irish National School Books, reprinted by Canadian publishers, which were authorized and in use in the schools for the next twenty years. These books, or readers, provided the curriculum and a method of dividing up the years of elementary education. The 1st or Junior Division used the First Book, the 2nd or Intermediate used the Second and Third Books, and the 3rd or Senior Division used the Fourth and Fifth Books.

Gradually, more subjects were added that were not directly addressed by the readers, including mechanics, chemistry, music, and drawing. By 1871 there were a total of nineteen subjects

EMPIRE DAY IN THE SCHOOLS

Empire Day (later Commonwealth Day) was commemo-
rated in Ontario schools on or close to 24 May, the Queen's
official birthday. An idea that originated with the strongly
patriotic Clementina (Trenholm) Fessenden (1843–1918),
Empire Day was first celebrated in 1898 in Dundas, Ontario.
The first official Empire Day in the schools was 23 May the
following year. It grew to become a full-day event and one
of the highlights of the school year. Until 1970, the schools
were provided with a detailed booklet containing the sug-
gested program, and readings and essays on the Empire and
the Royal Family.

An Empire Day that was felt to be especially important
was that in 1927, the Diamond Jubilee year for Canadian
Confederation. Below is the program for the day as envi-
sioned by the Education Department.

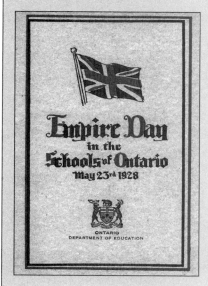

*The 1928 booklet for use in
the schools on Empire Day.*

OISE Library, OHEC Collection.

PROGRAMME

FORENOON

1. Opening Exercises — Psalm 96 and the Lord's Prayer.
2. Hymn — From Ocean Unto Ocean.
3. A Geography Lesson — Canada in 1867 and in 1927. (See maps in booklet.)
4. Song — The Maple Leaf.
5. Recitations or Readings — See History Manual, pages 102–10.
6. A School Song.
7. A History Lesson — A review of the British North America Act, noting the leaders in the Confederation movement, particularly Macdonald and Brown.
8. Selection on phonograph — Messages to the boys and girls from the King and Queen (Victor Record 245001A).
9. An Essay or Address — The Story of Confederation. (See 1927 booklet.)
10. School Song.
11. Decoration of Memorial Tablet or Monument.

AFTERNOON

1. Chairman's Address.
2. School Song.
3. Greetings from the Hon. G.H. Ferguson — Read by the teacher — (see booklet).
4. Recitation — "For Country and For King" (1927 booklet).

5. Patriotic Song or selection on phonograph.
6. An Essay or Address — "Canada, To-day and in Prospect."
7. Pageant representing phases in Canadian life or history.
8. Song — "O Canada."
9. Dramatization of "The Imperial Conference, 1926." (For suggestions see 1927 booklet, page 7.)

covered in the curriculum. But the poor state of training meant that the majority of teachers were unprepared to teach the variety of subjects required and much rote learning from the textbooks was the norm. In 1884, the number of subjects taught was cut back to twelve: reading, writing, arithmetic, history, geography, composition, grammar, music, drawing, temperance, drill and callisthenics, and agriculture. But, in a new departure, school boards now had the right to modify the curriculum to meet local needs.

Another revision took place in 1904 at the elementary level and again in 1920. But it was in 1937 that a truly progressive curriculum was introduced covering English, social studies, arithmetic, natural science, health education, music, and art. This 1937 course of study became popularly known as "The Grey Book" and continued in use until 1960.

It proved to be more difficult to direct and control what was taught at the high-school level. In the early years, education at the secondary level emphasized the study of Latin and Greek. The 1853 Grammar School Act gave the Council of Public Instruction the right to regulate the courses of study and the first attempt was made to reduce the emphasis on the classics and to add a more practical English and commercial education. This change in curriculum was not universally followed and in 1871 there was another attempt to give more weight to the study of English, mathematics, history, and geography, and to make provision for French, German, science, and commercial subjects.

As universities continued to require Latin and Greek for admission, however, change was slow. In 1921, the high-school course was reduced to five years and the number of compulsory courses was also reduced. In 1937, more changes were made to the curriculum, although not on the sweeping scale of the changes made at the elementary level. Following the 1968 publication of the Hall-Dennis Report, *Living and Learning*, massive changes were made at both levels.

Where to Find Ontario Curriculum Documents

The OHEC collection has a complete set of historical Ontario curriculum documents as do many other university libraries at institutions with faculties of education.

THE TEXTBOOKS OUR ANCESTORS USED

The scarcity of books in this Province is to be regretted by all lovers of learning. I am clearly of opinion [sic] that if any person would send into the States, or to England, for a collection not only of school books but of others, he would greatly benefit himself and the Province also.

— Richard Cockrel, *Thoughts on the Education of Youth* (Newark, U.C.: G. Tiffany, 1795), 14.

A page from the Primer for the Royal Canadian Reader Series. Toronto, Canada Publishing Company, 1883.

One of the best ways to gain an insight into the curriculum and the worldview of a child in early Ontario is to read the textbooks of the time. Far fewer books were available to young people growing up in the past than is the case today and the content of the books used in schools subsequently had a greater impact on young minds. The same small group of textbooks were often authorized for use for decades, meaning that more than one generation would have been familiar with and influenced by the same material. Even today, libraries with collections of historical textbooks have elderly visitors who simply want to look at the textbooks they remember so well from the past.

Students were particularly attached to what were generically known as "the readers"; as we have seen, these readers were used to define a pupil's progress through the school. The content of the readers typically covered reading, spelling, history, geography, and natural history. For over twenty years, from 1846–1868, the series of *Irish National School Books* that Ryerson had admired so much were almost the only books authorized for use in the schools. Other readers superseded those from Ireland eventually, when concern over more Canadian content became an issue; the *Canadian Readers,* the *Royal Readers,* the *Ontario Readers,* the *Treasury Readers,* and the *Life and Literature Series* in succession until 1949. The separate schools had their own authorized readers, for example, the *Canadian Catholic Readers.*

Beyond the readers, textbooks were approved for all the school subjects: agriculture, bookkeeping, civics, drawing, domestic science, English, geography, history, mathematics, music, religious studies, science, spelling, and writing. There were others authorized for what would be considered unusual subjects today; for example, temperance. Amusing, too, to modern eyes are texts such as *Health in the House: Twenty-Five Lectures on Elementary Physiology in Its Application to the Daily Wants of Man and Animals,*

SPELLERS AND GRAMMARS

Some of the earliest references to textbooks in Ontario are to spelling book or "spellers," as spelling was considered a key part of literacy and these books were available in many homes. Some that have been recorded as being used in the earliest days of schooling were American in origin, which helped to feed the unease felt about the influences from south of the border penetrating the schools.

Spellers were used not only as lists of words for drilling students but also as a means of instilling moral values and codes of behaviour in children. Later, they included elements of British and Canadian history and geography.

LESSONS IN WORDS OF ONE SYLLABLE

LESSON I.

I knew a nice girl, but she was not good: she was cross, and told fibs. One day she went out to take a walk in the fields, and tore her frock in a bush; and when she came home, she said she had not done it, but that the dog had done it with his paw. Was that good? — No.

—William Mavor, *The English Spelling Book…*
From the 241st London edition
(Toronto: Brewer, McPhail, 1853), 27.

Grammar was also thought to be of paramount importance in any good education and students spent many hours

A page from William Mavor's The English Spelling Book.... *Toronto: Brewer, McPhail, 1853.*

learning the parts of speech, parsing sentences, and learning lists of words with Latin roots. The example below is of work undertaken at the public school level; the high-school-level grammar was even more rigorous and detailed.

Definition — A **relative** pronoun is one that relates to an antecedent, and that joins it to a clause by way of describing or limiting it.

NOTE TO TEACHER: It is not essential, at this stage, to keep before young pupils the difference between a clause that *limits*, and one that *describes*. If, however, the teacher chooses to do so, he may show that a clause *limits* when it distinguishes its antecedent from all other objects of the same name: thus, THE SOLDIER WHO WAS WOUNDED HAS RECOVERED; and that a clause *describes* when it does not do this: thus, TORONTO, WHICH IS THE CAPITAL OF ONTARIO, IS IN YORK COUNTY. Here, of course, as elsewhere in the book, the minuteness of the matter taken up must depend on the intelligence of the class.

— *The Public School Grammar....*
(Toronto: Canada Publishing Co., 1886), 65.

Delivered to the Wives and Children of Working-Men in Leeds and Saltaire, by Catherine Buckton, which was authorized for use from 1877 to 1886, and *Hygiene for Young People,* by A.P. Knight, authorized from 1914 to 1919.

The Authorization of Textbooks in Ontario

In the early days of Ontario schooling there were few books available for pupils to use in the schools and no fixed idea that all the pupils should be using the same text. Instead, whatever textbooks were on hand were used, which meant an eclectic mix of English- and American-published materials. The lack of uniform texts became a source of complaint from teachers and the use of American texts caused unease in a province that was already apprehensive about the American influence on Canada.

In 1846, as we have seen, Ryerson began the process of prescribing what texts could be used in the classroom, and by the time he retired in 1876 there were fifty-five books on the authorized list for elementary schools, almost all with a Canadian or English copyright. Authorization of high-schools texts followed more slowly.

In the first years of authorization, lists of approved texts appeared in the *Journal of Education for Upper Canada.* When this publication ceased in 1877, the Department of Education began to send out a circular containing both lists of approved and recommended textbooks and the regulations for their use. This became known as Circular 14 and continued to be sent annually to the schools until 1993. The current list for classes from kindergarten to Grade 12 is known as the Trillium List (*www.edu.gov.on.ca/trilliumlist*).

In the nineteenth century, authorization meant the exclusive use of approved textbooks in the classroom. Failure to do so meant a loss of a portion of the education grant to a school board, an amount which the board could deduct from the salary of the offending teacher. Increasingly, however, supplementary materials were added to the authorized lists so that local schools could make some independent decisions. The cost of the textbooks was generally borne by the pupils themselves.

Ontario Teachers' Manuals

Textbooks were not only provided for the student; manuals were also published to be used by teachers as a guide to teaching the curriculum, with subjects ranging from agriculture, horticulture, and nature study to grammar and sewing. These make interesting reading for those who have teachers in their family as they provide precise details on what was expected of the teacher and what and how a subject should be taught. Many of these manuals are available on the Internet Archive or on Google Books.

Further Reading

Baldus, Bernd, and Kassam, Meenaz. "'Make Me Truthful Good and Mild': Values in Nineteenth-Century Ontario Schoolbooks." *Canadian Journal of Sociology* 21, no. 3 (Summer 1996), 327–58.

Marling, Alexander. *A Brief History of Public and High School Textbooks Authorized for the Province of Ontario, 1846–1889.* Toronto: Warwick, 1890.

Parvin, Viola Elizabeth. *Authorization of Textbooks for the Schools of Ontario.* Toronto: Published in Association with the Canadian Textbook Publishers Institute by University of Toronto Press, 1965. See particularly her "Bibliography of Elementary School Textbooks Authorized for Use in Ontario Schools from 1846–1950."

White, E.T. *Public School Text-Books in Ontario.* London, ON: Chas. Chapman, 1922. Internet Archive.

Libraries with Collections of Historical Textbooks

The OHEC collection has a complete set of Ontario textbooks authorized since 1846 and a number of others known to have been used in the schools before that time. Other faculty of education libraries have extensive collections, including Queen's University, the University of Western Ontario, and Lakehead University. The Internet Archive is also an excellent source for old textbooks.

Archives of Ontario RG 2

RG 2-34 Minutes of the Committee to Revise the National Readers and the List of Text Books for Common and Grammar Schools, 1866–1868.

Ontario. Department of Education. *Textbooks Approved or Recommended for Use in Elementary and Secondary Schools* (Circular 14). Toronto: The Department, 1887–1993.

CHAPTER 6

Post-Secondary Education

Lieutenant-Governor Simcoe spoke, shortly after his arrival, of the need for a university in the new colony. The Scottish-born John Strachan, clergyman and schoolmaster, who arrived in Upper Canada three years after Simcoe had left the country, shared his view that a university was necessary to maintain British values and the established social order. Both men believed that the Church of England was the de facto established church of Upper Canada and that any university should be strongly tied to this church — a view not held by all. Strachan travelled to England and, in 1827, returned with a Royal Charter for the University of King's College, the province's first university.

If the university or college attended by an ancestor is not known, it may be useful to begin a search by examining the records of the institution that was either closest to the family home or was affiliated with the family's church. There were relatively few universities in the nineteenth century: the University of Toronto (and the colleges and universities federated with it), Queen's University in Kingston, McMaster University, first in Toronto and then Hamilton, the University of Ottawa, and the University of Western Ontario.

The best source for information on students at Ontario's universities is each institution's own archives. In addition to the original records of student admissions and graduations each university may still hold, university yearbooks are a useful source of information. Many contain photographs of graduates and short descriptions of their educational history to date. Some universities also publish alumni directories that allow graduates to be traced in later life.

Also search the library catalogue of each institution for publications other than the general histories provided in the following section. Lists of names in a variety of publications can be unearthed in this way, as can be seen in the list of publications associated with each university.

University of Toronto

Although Strachan had obtained a royal charter for the University of King's College in 1827, political difficulties and a lack of money delayed the opening of this university until 1843. On 31 December 1849, the Church of England–controlled King's College ceased to exist, succeeded the following day by the non-denominational University of Toronto.

University of Toronto Archives: *www.library.utoronto.ca/utarms.*

Alumni cards —— information on graduates and former students. Applications to enter the university, 1906–1958, completed by the students themselves. A finding aid is available.

Course and prize lists, up until 1913.

Press clipping files, 1890–1970s, on individual students.

Large collection of early photographs of sports teams, etc.

Friedland, Martin L. *The University of Toronto: A History.* Toronto: University of Toronto Press, 2002.

Alexander, W.J. *The University of Toronto and Its Colleges, 1827– 1906.* Toronto: The University Library, published by the Librarian, 1906. Internet Archive.

Wallace, W. Stewart. "The Graduates of Kings College, Toronto." *Ontario History* 42, no. 3 (1950), 163–64.

Fasti Academici: Annals of King's College, Toronto, Containing Lists of the Officers and Members of the University, and of the Students Who Obtained Certificates of Honour, Prizes, or Scholarships. From 1827 to 1849. Toronto: H. Rowsell, 1850.

University of Toronto. *University of Toronto Roll of War Service, 1914–1918.* Toronto: University of Toronto Press, 1921.

Torontoensis, 1898–1966: The University of Toronto graduate year-book lists faculty and graduating students and includes many student photographs of societies, committees, and sports teams. Later issues have a photograph of each graduate. As each college federated with the university, their graduates were included in *Torontoensis.*

Victoria University in the University of Toronto

Victoria College, established in 1841, was originally founded in Cobourg as the Upper Canada Academy by the Wesleyan Methodist Church. In 1884, Victoria College and Albert University (established in Belleville as Albert College in 1857) merged to become

Victoria University. In 1890, Victoria University became federated with the University of Toronto, moving from Cobourg to Toronto in 1892.

Victoria University in the University of Toronto Archives: *library. vicu.utoronto.ca/vu*. The archives has an extensive collection of early student records, including those for Upper Canada Academy and Albert College.

Sissons, C.B. *A History of Victoria University*. Toronto: University of Toronto Press, 1952.

"Victoria University." *Canada Educational Monthly* 1 (November 1879), 195–96. Includes examination results and a list of the matriculating entrants and their high schools or other places of education.

Trinity College in the University of Toronto

After the University of Toronto replaced King's College in 1850, John Strachan set about once again to establish a university that would be affiliated with the Church of England. Trinity College opened in 1852 on Queen Street in Toronto. The college was federated with the University of Toronto in 1904.

Trinity College Archives: *www.trinity.utoronto.ca/Library_Archives/ Archives*.

The Calendar of University of Trinity College, Toronto..., 1853 to 1928. Lists of faculty, students, and prize-winners.

The Degree Book, 1853–1904. A listing of all graduates; after

1904 the listing is for divinity graduates only. After 1904, other student records are at the University of Toronto Archives.

File cards, late nineteenth century to the 1970s — graduates and others who attended the college. The information on each card varies.

Class photographs from the late nineteenth century to the present.

Reed, T.A. *A History of the University of Trinity College, Toronto, 1852–1952.* Toronto: University of Toronto Press, 1952.

Young, A.H., and W.A. Kirkwood. *The War Memorial Volume of Trinity College, Toronto.* Toronto: Printers' Guild, 1922.

The University of Trinity College Toronto. *Directory of Graduates and Other Alumni.* Toronto: The Corporation of Trinity College, 1930.

University of St. Michael's College, University of Toronto

St. Michael's College was established in 1852 by the Basilian Fathers to educate Roman Catholic students. It was federated with the University of Toronto in 1910.

University of St. Michael's College Archives: *www.utoronto.ca/ stmikes/archives/index.html.* The University of St. Michael's College Archives holds student records from 1852.

A Register of Graduates in Arts 1920 to 1940, St. Michael's College in the University of Toronto. Compiled by Robert Joseph Scollard. Toronto: University of St. Michael's College Archives, 1981. Similar registers have been published for graduates up until 1969.

Seventy-Fifth Anniversary, St. Michael's College in the University of Toronto. Toronto: St. Michael's College, 1927.

University College, University of Toronto

University College was founded in 1853 as "the provincial college" to provide a higher education without religious affiliation.

Bissell, Claude Thomas. *University College: A Portrait, 1853–1953.* Toronto: University of Toronto Press, 1953.

The Calendar of the University of Toronto and University College..., *1887–1910.* [Some issues have title: *The Calendar of University College, Toronto...*] CIHM microfiche series, no A02103.

Fasti from 1850 to 1887. Compiled and edited by W.J. Loudon and W.F. Maclean. Toronto: Williamson, 1887. Contains a directory of graduates' current residences.

Queen's University

Queen's was established in Kingston in 1841 by the Church of Scotland.

Queen's University Archives: *archives.queensu.ca.* The Queen's University Archives has a searchable online database of its holdings. Student registers are available from 1842 to 1907.

Calvin, Delano Dexter. *Queen's University at Kingston: The First Century of a Scottish-Canadian Foundation, 1841–1941.* Kingston, ON: Trustees of the University, 1941.

Overseas Record: Record of Graduates, Alumni, Members of Staff, and Students of Queen's University on Active Military (Overseas) Service (to June 1st, 1917). Kingston, ON: Queen's University, 1914–1917.

McMaster University

Located in Hamilton since 1930, McMaster University was first established in Toronto in 1887 by the Baptist Convention of Ontario. The original Toronto building now houses the Royal Conservatory of Music. Most of the records of the university for the years before 1957, when it became a public university, are housed in the Canadian Baptist Archives in the McMaster Divinity College.

Canadian Baptist Archives: *www.macdiv.ca/students/baptistarchives.php.*

Johnston, Charles M. *McMaster University.* Toronto: Published for McMaster University by University of Toronto Press, 1976. Two volumes.

Woodstock College Memorial Book. Toronto: The Memorial Committee, Woodstock College Alumni Association, 1951. Contains a list of all known former pupils of this college, which was one of the precursors to McMaster University, including their war service and their residences at the time of publication, if known.

University of Ottawa

The College of Bytown was founded in 1848 as a bilingual Roman Catholic institution. In 1861 it became the College of Ottawa , and in 1866, after receiving the necessary royal charter it was transformed into the University of Ottawa. The University of Ottawa Archives does not retain student records.

Prevost, Michel. *The University of Ottawa Since 1848*. Ottawa, ON: University of Ottawa, 2008.

University of Western Ontario

Western was founded in 1878 as The Western University of London Ontario. This institution incorporated Huron University College, the Anglican theological school, which had been established in 1863.

University of Western Ontario Archives: *www.lib.uwo.ca/archives*. Talman, James J. *Huron College, 1863–1963*. London, ON: Huron College, 1963.

Talman, James, and Ruth Davis Talman. *"Western," 1878–1953: Being the History of the Origins and Development of the University of Western Ontario, During Its First Seventy-Five Years*. London, ON: University of Western Ontario, 1973.

Other Lists of Students and Faculty

Hodgins, Thomas, ed. *The Canada Educational Directory and Calendar for 1857–8…*. Toronto: Maclear & Co., 1857. For Upper Canada, lists officials in the Education Department and the Council of Public Instruction; teachers at the normal and model schools; the Chairman of Trustees and the headmaster of the grammar schools; the local superintendents of common schools; officials, graduates, and undergraduates at the University of Toronto; professors at University College, Toronto; University of Trinity College, Toronto — professors, graduates, and undergraduates; Principal and Master at Upper Canada College, Toronto; professors, graduates, and students at the University of Victoria College, Cobourg;

professors and graduates at University of Queen's College, Kingston; professors only listed for Regiopolis College (Kingston), Knox College (Toronto), Bytown College (Ottawa), St. Michael's College (Toronto), and the Toronto School of Medicine. CIHM microfiche series, no. 22636.

Marling, Alexander. The *Canada Educational Directory and Year Book for 1876*... CIHM microfiche series, no. 08518.

Further Reading

Keane, David. "Rediscovering Ontario University Students of the Mid Nineteenth Century: Sources for and Approaches to the Study of the Experience of Going to College and Personal, Family and Social Backgrounds of Students." Ph.D. dissertation, University of Toronto, 1981. Four volumes. Although this dissertation was written over twenty-five years ago, it remains an invaluable resource for those looking to find what student lists are available for the universities of mid-nineteenth-century Ontario.

McKillop, A.B. *Matters of the Mind: The University in Ontario, 1791–1951*. Ontario Historical Studies series. Toronto: University of Toronto Press, 1994.

Read, Donald E. "University Yearbooks as a Source of Migration." *Families* 24, no. 4 (1985), 225–27.

APPENDIX

Schoolhouse Museums in Ontario

Bogarttown Schoolhouse
14732 Woodbine Avenue
Gormley, ON L0H 1G0
www.townofws.com/museum.asp

Brockston County School Museum
2719 Vivian Line 37
Stratford, ON N5A 5E1
search.informationperth.ca/record/PER0102

Buxton National Historic Site and Museum
21975 A.D. Shadd Road
North Buxton, ON N0P 1Y0
www.buxtonmuseum.com

Cumberland Heritage Village Museum
2940 Old Montreal Road
Cumberland, ON K4C 1E6
ottawa.ca/residents/heritage/museums/cumberland/index_en.html

Enoch Turner Schoolhouse
106 Trinity Street
Toronto, ON M5A 3C6
www.enochturnerschoolhouse.ca

Frontenac County Schools Museum
414 Regent Street, Kingston
ON K7K 3E1
www.fcsmuseum.com

Heritage Schoolhouse Museum
(York Region District School Board)
8820 Woodbine Avenue
Markham, ON L3R 0E5
heritage.schoolhouse@yrdsb.edu.on.ca

Historic Zion Schoolhouse
1091 Finch Avenue East
Toronto, ON M2H 1S8
www.toronto.ca/culture/museums/zion-schoolhouse.htm

The Little Schoolhouse and Museum
South Baymouth, Manitoulin Island, ON
www.manitoulin-island.com/museums/little_schoolhouse.htm

Old Britannia School House (Peel Board of Education)
5576 Hurontario Street
Mississauga, ON L5R 1B3
www.britanniaschoolhousefriends.org

School House Museum
35753 Highway 7
Deep River, ON K0J 1P0
bright-ideas-software.com/Schoolhouse

School House, Black Creek Pioneer Village
1000 Murray Ross Parkway
Toronto, ON M3J 2P3
www.blackcreek.ca

School House, Lang Pioneer Village
104 Lang Road
Keene, ON K0L 2G0
www.langpioneervillage.ca

School House, Upper Canada Village
13740 County Road 2
Morrisburg, ON K0C 1X0
www.uppercanadavillage.com/tour22.htm

**Sesquicentennial Museum and Archives and
Century Schoolhouse (Toronto District School Board)**
263 McCaul Street
Toronto, ON M5T 1P6
toes.tdsb.on.ca/day/tusc

Thames Valley Museum School
656 Main Street
Burgessville, ON N0J 1C0
www.museumschool.ca

Victoria School Museum, Carleton Place
267 Edmund St.
Carleton Place, ON K7C 3E8
www.victoriaschoolmuseum.com

Victorian Classroom, Suddaby Public School
171 Frederick Street
Kitchener, ON N2H 2M6
brant.smith@sympatico.ca

Wilson MacDonald Memorial School Museum
3513 Rainham Road
Selkirk, ON N0A 1P0
haldimand.cioc.ca/record/SIM1552

Additional Works Consulted

Acts Relating to the Education Department, Public and High Schools and Truancy, Ontario. Toronto: King's Printer, 1901.

Bishop, Olga. *Publications of the Government of Ontario, 1867–1900.* Toronto: Ministry of Government Services, 1976.

———. *Publications of the Government of the Province of Canada, 1841–1867.* Ottawa: National Library of Canada, 1963.

———. *Publications of the Province of Upper Canada and of Great Britain Relating to Upper Canada, 1791–1840.* Toronto: Ontario Ministry of Citizenship and Culture, 1984.

Cochrane, Jean. *The One-Room School in Canada.* Calgary: Fifth House Publishers, 2001.

Cockrel, Richard. *Thoughts on the Education of Youth.* Newark, U.C.: G. Tiffany, 1795.

Finley, E.G. *Education in Canada: A Bibliography.* Toronto: Dundurn Press, 1989.

Gervais, Gaetan. *The Bibliography of Ontario History, 1976–1986.* Toronto: Dundurn Press, 1989.

Gidney, R.D. "Elementary Education in Upper Canada: A Reassessment." *Ontario History* 65 (September 1973): 169–85.

Gilchrist, J. Brian. *Inventory of Ontario Newspapers, 1793–1986.* Toronto: Micromedia, 1987.

Graham, Elizabeth. "Schoolmarms and Early Teaching in Ontario." In *Women at Work: Ontario, 1850–1930.* Toronto: Canadian Women's Educational Press, 1974.

Harris, Robin. *A History of Higher Education in Canada, 1663–1960.* Toronto: University of Toronto Press, 1976.

Harris, Robin and Tremblay, Arthur. *A Bibliography of Higher Education in Canada.* Toronto: University of Toronto Press, 1960.

Houston, Susan E. and Alison Prentice. *Schooling and Scholars in Nineteenth-Century Ontario.* Toronto: University of Toronto Press, 1988.

Jameson, Anna. *Winter Studies and Summer Rambles in Canada,* London: Saunders and Otley, 1838. ECO.

Langton, H.H. *A Gentlewoman in Upper Canada: The Journals of Anne Langton.* Toronto: Clarke, Irwin, 1950.

Logan, Anne M. *School's Out: A Pictorial History of Ontario's Converted Schoolhouses.* Erin, ON: Boston Mills Press, 1987.

McMurrich, William Barclay. *The School Laws of Ontario....* Toronto: Goodwin, 1894. Internet Archive.

Phillips, Charles Edward. *The Development of Education in Canada.* Toronto: Gage, 1957.

Ross, George W. *The School System of Ontario (Canada): Its History and Distinctive Features.* New York: D. Appleton, 1896. Internet Archive.

Schuessler, Karl and Mary. *School on Wheels: Reaching and Teaching the Isolated Children of the North*. Erin, ON: Boston Mills Press, 1986.

Spragge, George W. "Monitorial Schools in the Canadas, 1810–1845." Doctor of Pedagogy dissertation, University of Toronto, 1935.

Stamp, Robert M. "Empire Day in the Schools of Ontario: The Training of Young Imperialists." *Journal of Canadian Studies* 8, no. 3 (1973), 32–42.

Thomas, Clara. *Ryerson of Upper Canada*. Toronto: Ryerson Press, 1969.

Wilkinson, Margaret Ann. *Genealogy and the Law in Canada*. Toronto: OGS/Dundurn Press, 2010.

Wilson, J. Donald. "The Teacher in Early Ontario." In *Aspects of Nineteenth Century Ontario: Essays Presented to James J. Talman*, edited by F.H. Armstrong, H.A. Stevenson, and J.D. Wilson. Toronto: University of Toronto Press in association with the University of Western Ontario, 1974: 218–36.

OTHER GENEALOGIST'S
REFERENCE SHELF TITLES

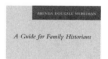

CRIME AND PUNISHMENT IN UPPER CANADA
A Researcher's Guide
Janice Nickerson
978-1-55488-770-5 $19.99

This reference provides genealogists and social historians with context and tools to locate sources on criminal activity and its consequences for the Upper Canada period (1791–1841) of Ontario's history. An entertaining, educational read, it features chapters with detailed inventories of available records in federal, provincial, and local repositories; published and online transcripts and indices; and suggestions for additional reading.

GENEALOGICAL STANDARDS OF EVIDENCE
A Guide for Family Historians
Brenda Dougall Merriman
978-1-55488-451-3 $19.99

This guide takes readers through the genealogical process of research and identification, along the way examining how the genealogical community has developed standards of evidence and documentation, what the standards are, and how they can be applied. A perfect supplement to courses, workshops, and seminars, this book provides an in-depth reference perfect for compiling and checking notes.

CONSERVING, PRESERVING, AND RESTORING YOUR HERITAGE: A Professional's Advice

Conserving,
Preserving,
and Restoring
Your Heritage

Kennis Kim

978-1-55488-462-9 $19.99

Our family history may be held in documents, photographs, books, clothing, or textiles; sometimes complete collections of items such as coins, trading cards, or stamps. As custodians of pieces of our history, we are faced with how to maintain these items. Here's all you need to determine what you can do yourself to preserve your precious things for future generations.

GENEALOGY AND THE LAW IN CANADA

Genealogy
and the Law
in Canada

Dr. Margaret Ann Wilkinson

978-1-55488-452-0 $19.99

The development of digital records and broad access to the web has revolutionized the ways in which genealogists approach their investigations — and has made it much easier to locate relevant information. The law, on the other hand, remains very connected to particular geographic locations. This book discusses the relevant laws — access to information, protection of personal data, and copyright — applicable to those working within Canada with materials that are located in Canada.

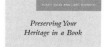

PUBLISH YOUR FAMILY HISTORY:
Preserving Your Heritage in a Book
Susan Yates and Greg Ioannou
978-1-55488-727-9 $19.99

Many people want to write a family history, but few ever take on the job of publishing one. *Publish Your Family History* will tell you all the fundamentals of book production, together with the important details that distinguish a home-published book from a homemade one.

Available at your favourite bookseller.

Visit www.dundurn.com for
reviews, videos, updates, and more!